Meant to Last

Paul E. Steele & Charles C. Ryrie

While this book is designed for the reader's personal
enjoyment, it is also intended for group study. A
Leader's Guide with Victor Multiuse Transparency
Masters is available from your local bookstore or
from the publisher.

VICTOR ──────────

BOOKS a division of SP Publications, Inc.
WHEATON, ILLINOIS 60187

Offices also in
Whitby, Ontario, Canada
Amersham-on-the-Hill, Bucks, England

Unless otherwise noted, Scripture quotations are from the *New American Standard Bible* © 1960, 1962, 1968, 1971, 1972, 1973 by The Lockman Foundation, La Habra, California. Other quotations are from the *New International Version* (NIV), © 1978 by the New York International Bible Society; the *King James Version* (KJV); *The New Testament in Modern English* (PH), © J.B. Phillips 1958, The Macmillan Company. Used by permission.

Recommended Dewey Decimal Classification: 241
  Suggested Subject Heading: MARRIAGE, DIVORCE, AND REMARRIAGE

Library of Congress Catalog Card Number: 83-060814
ISBN: 0-88207-385-0

VICTOR BOOKS
A division of SP Publications, Inc.
        Wheaton, Illinois 60187

Contents

Preface   The Divorce Generation   **4**
1   What Is Marriage?   **7**
2   God's Purposes for Marriage   **17**
3   Is Headship a Hardship?   **29**
4   Christ, a Man's Example   **41**
5   Keys to Harmony   **49**
6   What's Forever For?   **59**
7   Satan's Strategy   **73**
8   A Survey of Divorce Views   **85**
9   Probing the Views on Divorce   **99**
10   Happiness Is . . .   **119**
11   Reconciliation   **129**
12   The Divorced Person in the Church   **143**

Preface

The Divorce Generation

Like Louis Carroll's Alice, we find ourselves in a topsy-turvy world where everything is upside down and backwards. This condition is nothing new. The Word of the Lord through Isaiah the Prophet invoked a stern warning upon those "that call evil good, and good evil; that put darkness for light, and light for darkness; that put bitter for sweet, and sweet for bitter!" (Isaiah 5:20, KJV)

The spirit of our age is that of twisted values and distorted ideals, where the characteristics of 2 Timothy 3 and Romans 1 have become the norm, where secularism seeks to usurp God's truth, and where rationalization has largely replaced revelation as the criterion upon which judgments are made.

At a time like this, the church is always faced with the peril of selling its birthright for a mess of pottage. Satan, masquerading as an angel of light, is seeking to deceive believers into accepting counterfeit ideas. When man does accept his lie, Satan is adept at devising new ways of justifying conduct standards that are clearly contrary to God's righteous character. When given enough time, these views sometimes become the "traditional" view of the church, "teaching for doctrines the commandments of men" (Matthew 15:9, KJV).

Perhaps the area where this deterioration of God's best is most clearly seen is in the matter of marriage, divorce, and remarriage. The last thirty years have been called the Space Age and the Now Generation. Perhaps they should be called The Divorce Generation.

Twentieth-century American divorce statistics are staggering. From a 1920 figure of one divorce in seven marriages to an incredible 1977 statistic of one in two, America is rapidly approaching a record two million divorces each year. In some counties in California, more people are being divorced each year than are being married. We have become the Divorce Generation.

Where is the church in all of this? In the middle 1960s when the divorce rate was becoming one in three, one major denomination published a study which revealed that in church-related homes the divorce figure was one in 4,000. In the turbulent years from 1965 to 1980, the church moved from a bedrock of stability to the shifting sands of compromise. Caught up in the move toward independence and selfish indulgence, the church has changed its value system, producing not only an alarming divorce rate in church-related homes, but also an unprecedented number of divorces among evangelicals and their leaders.

Moody Monthly reported that the divorce rate among evangelicals is fast catching up with the national average (Cynthia Scott, "Divorce Dilemma," September 1981, p. 7). The seeds for this precipitous situation were planted long ago when justification was made for divorces in what seemed to be "rare" or "exceptional" cases. Now we are reaping a harvest that will affect the church for generations to come.

All of this sounds pessimistic, and it should. The situation today is grim, but there is hope. That hope lies in conforming to God's standards as He has revealed them in His Word. To do this, we must know what they are, and then obey them explicitly, without changing, diluting, or obscuring them.

Marriage was God's idea and He is pleased with it. He has not given up on the home; it is still the foundation of any stable society. Marriage is not a man-made product, but a creation of God, instituted and honored by Him who does all things well, to bring happiness to mankind.

The modern church's loose attitude toward divorce, and its subsequent devaluation of marriage, clearly has failed to provide the stability and fulfillment God intends. The situation is worsening each day. It is time that we return to the principles given to us by God in His Word. When all else fails, read the directions. If we do, there is hope for The Divorce Generation.

Paul E. Steele
Charles C. Ryrie
1983

1

What Is Marriage?

Jim was a quiet, well-mannered young man who had been raised in an evangelical church in another town. He had accepted Christ as Saviour as a child and had only recently moved to California. He was dating an attractive young lady in our church and had of late been pressuring her to move in with him. She asked that he seek counseling.

His words were typical of the rationale pastors are hearing increasingly: "Why should we get married? What difference does a piece of paper make as long as we are in love? What is marriage anyway?"

The U.S. Census Bureau recorded one million unmarried cohabiting couples in 1979,[1] but some see this as only the tip of the iceberg, since many such couples do not register. Eleanor D. Macklin, in an article in *Psychology Today*,[2] estimates that up to 36 percent of university students live together, depending on the campus.

Terms such as "trial marriage," "limited unions," "contract marriage," "creative marriage," and "living together" are a part of the vocabulary that has rewritten the definition of modern marriage in this divorce generation.

What is marriage? Does the Bible provide us with a clear definition and description of marriage, divine style? The answer is an unqualified yes. Woven into the fabric of the biblical account of God's dealings with man are all the ingredients necessary to answer the questions regarding marriage.

What Marriage Is Not

Perhaps we should begin by discussing what marriage is not. Living together or consummating the physical relationship does *not* in itself constitute marriage.

When Christ encountered the woman of Samaria, He asked her to go and call her husband. She denied that she had a husband and Christ countered with these words: "You have well said, 'I have no husband'; for you have had five husbands; and the one whom you now have is not your husband" (John 4:17-18). In other words, though she was living with a man and having sexual relations with him, this did not constitute a marriage.

There are those today who purport the idea that when two people have a sexual relationship they become one flesh and that this is recognized by God as constituting marriage. Such an idea cannot be supported from Scripture.

The sexual relationship does constitute a part of the "one flesh" concept. The Apostle Paul asked, "Do you not know that the one who joins himself to a harlot is one body with her? For He says, 'The two will become one flesh'" (1 Corinthians 6:16). Physical union, however, is only one facet of what it means to be one flesh.

Bill Heth, in an important article on divorce and remarriage says, "The relationship which the 'one flesh' denotes does, of course, include the sexual aspect, but it includes far more than that."[3]

This idea is explicit in the scholarly works of Abel Isaksson and Gordon Wenham, where the one-flesh concept is shown to establish a "kinship" or "close relation" so that there is, so to speak, a horizontal "blood" relationship between the individuals themselves similar to the vertical blood relationship that exists between parents and children.[4 and 5]

To become someone's "flesh" was a common expression used to denote kinship (Genesis 29:12-14; 37:27; Judges 9:2; 2 Samuel 19:13). Isaksson concludes that it is reasonable to translate "flesh" in Genesis 2:24 by the word "relation." A. P. Ross says, "To become one flesh means becoming a spiritual, moral, intellectual, and physical unity."[6]

Another proof that sexual union does not constitute marriage is the fact that the Old Testament makes a clear distinction between a man's concubines and his wife or wives (Genesis 22:24; Judges 8:30-31; 2 Samuel 3:7; 5:13; 1 Kings 11:3). Thus we see that engaging in a sexual relationship does not constitute marriage.

Even more conclusive is the fact that sex outside the marriage bond is always considered sin in Scripture. "For fornicators and adulterers God will judge" (Hebrews 13:4). Deuteronomy 22:23-30 touches on a variety of cases involving sex before marriage. In some, the penalty was death. In certain others, the couple were to marry. But in every case premarital sex was clearly regarded as sin, even though sometimes the couple were forced to marry after the sin had been committed, and without the possibility of divorce (Deuteronomy 22:29). Clearly their promiscuity did not constitute marriage (Exodus 22:16-17).

Heading the list of the works of the flesh in Galatians 5:19 are sexual immorality and impurity. Sexual immorality is the first in the list of unrighteous acts listed in 1 Corinthians 6:9-10. Remember also 1 Thessalonians 4:7: "For God has not called us for the purpose of impurity, but in sanctification."

The Elements of Marriage
How can we answer Jim's question, "What is marriage anyway?" or Bob's similar question? Bob was a young man who had

a live-in girlfriend and he wanted to justify his situation. He inquired, "Where do we get the idea that we have to go through a ceremony and register with the state in order to be married in the eyes of God? We had our own ceremony privately and we are just as married as anyone else."

His question motivated us to research marriage customs, both biblical and extrabiblical (from Alfred Edersheim to Emily Post). In all societies, two people are married when their relationship is legally recognized to be marriage; but from a biblical perspective, there is much more involved than mere legal registration.

1. Mutual consent. It is clear that the man and woman involved must agree to join together in the marriage relationship. Marriage customs differ from time to time, and from place to place, but the parents of the man and woman should be involved in the choice to a greater or lesser degree. Greater involvement includes "arranged marriages" (Genesis 21:21; 34:4-6; Joshua 15:16; Judges 14:2-3; and lesser involves parental consent or "giving away" of the bride (1 Corinthians 7:37-38).

2. Some form of marriage agreement. This form differs in various cultures, but a contract seems to be a common element in all valid marriages. In some societies it involves a dowry (Genesis 34:12), sometimes referred to as "bride's wealth." In others the contract is informal and unwritten, but there is some kind of a commitment made before witnesses and validated in a legal way.

3. Conformity to certain social customs. There must be a rendering to Caesar the things that are Caesar's, a recognition of God-ordained authority (Matthew 22:21; Romans 13:1). In some cultures this has meant the proof of virginity; in others, a priority of marriage (Deuteronomy 22:13-17; Genesis 29:25-26). In our culture, marriage involves a marriage license, blood tests, and the subsequent registering of a valid marriage certificate. A marriage without this legal process is not recognized as legal in our society.

4. Consummation of the physical union. In 1 Corinthians 7:1-6, Paul emphasized that single people are not to live as though they are married: "It is good for a man not to touch a woman." Then he points out that married people are not to live as though they are single: "Let the husband fulfill his duty to his wife, and likewise also the wife to her husband." Paul continues to describe the withholding of sexual union as depriving or defrauding. Most cultures recognize that when one party refuses to consummate the relationship, the marriage may be annulled. (Exceptional cases where it is impossible physically to consummate a union can still be valid marriages with the agreement and understanding of both partners.)

The Covenant of Marriage
God says that marriage is to be held in honor among all (Hebrews 13:4). To despise it is to hold a view that is contrary to God's. Because God honors marriage and because people agree to a commitment in marriage, the covenant of marriage is sacred and binding in God's sight.

No passage in the Bible underscores this more forcibly than Malachi 2:13-16. The people of that day were bringing their offerings to the temple, but God did not accept them. They asked why, apparently not realizing that their sin had separated them from God. What sin? The sin of divorce. Notice some ramifications of divorce in this passage.

1. It broke fellowship with God so that He did not accept their sacrifices and offerings.

2. It unmasked the treachery of those men who in divorcing their wives broke their covenant, their agreement, or their word. These were long-standing marriages in which there had been real companionship, but divorce had ended all that (v. 14).

3. These divorces affected the families, making it difficult to insure godly descendants (v. 15). It is also possible that the first part of verse 15 is saying that since God made only one wife for Adam (though He had power to make two or more, had He

chosen to do so), to divorce and remarry, as some of the Israelites were doing, violated that original creation pattern, since
such a man would become a two-woman man, rather than the
one-woman man God intended.

4. To divorce is to do something God hates because it treats
the divorced mate with cruelty (v. 16). In his book, *To Have and
to Hold,* David Atkinson writes:

> By covenant is meant an agreement between two parties based
> on promise which includes these four elements. First: an under-
> taking of committed faithfulness made by one party to the other
> (or by each to the other). Secondly, the acceptance of that
> undertaking by the other party; thirdly, public knowledge of
> such an undertaking and its acceptance; fourthly, the growth
> of a personal relationship based on and expressive of such a
> commitment.[7]

The marriage covenant finds analogies in God's covenant
with Israel and His covenant with the church. The prophets
Hosea, Jeremiah, Ezekiel, and Isaiah repeatedly used the analo-
gy of marriage and the language of the covenant to describe
God's persistent pursuit of Israel, in spite of her unfaithfulness.
God, bound by unconditional covenants with Israel, promised
to keep them in spite of her persistent harlotry and spiritual
adultery.

Also analogous to a husband's relationship with his wife in
marriage is Christ's relationship with the church (Ephesians
5:18-33). The covenantal nature of the marriage relationship
is expressed in the marriage vows.

In my wedding services I do not use the traditional vows or
service; I write each service with the specific couple in mind and
use a carefully worded set of vows that I have worked out using
biblical criteria. I ask each party individually to commit him or
herself to all that Scripture requires in the relationship. Included are the words: "I understand that marriage is a covenant
which cannot be broken and God is a witness of this oath."

It was my privilege to perform such a wedding service for a Christian couple a number of years ago. After the ceremony, an uncle of the bride approached me and asked if I had ever studied law. I assured him that I had not. He then informed me that he was an attorney and something of an expert on contract law. He said, "I have never heard such an airtight contract as you required of that couple. If a divorce court were to take into account what has been agreed to here today, there never could be legal justification for divorce."

I replied that permanence in the marriage was always my goal, because it is God's. God never takes vows lightly.

> If a man makes a vow to the Lord, or takes an oath to bind himself with a binding obligation, he shall not violate his word; he shall do according to all that proceeds out of his mouth (Numbers 30:2; see also Deuteronomy 23:21 and Ecclesiastes 5:4).

If someone argues that vows are only words, he should remember the words of Christ:

> And I say to you, that every careless word that men shall speak, they shall render account for it in the day of judgment. For by your words you shall be justified, and by your words you shall be condemned (Matthew 12:36-37).

If God takes our idle words seriously, how much more He regards our vows taken before Him as sacred commitments! Marriage is a covenant that should never be broken. Writing to Timothy, Paul spoke of an apostate age that would be marked by an unprecedented selfishness (2 Timothy 3:1-5). Among the eighteen words used to describe one who exemplifies this age is a Greek word translated in the KJV "trucebreakers." The NASB preferred the word "irreconcilable" and the NIV "unforgiving." Some have suggested "implacable." Basically, it means a person who refuses to enter into a covenant. In Romans 1:31,

Paul gives a similar list and uses a different but related word. It is translated "covenantbreakers" (KJV), "untrustworthy" (NASB), and "faithless" (NIV). It means refusing to abide by covenants made. If an apostate age, when man has turned from God, is characterized by those who either refuse to enter into a covenant or refuse to keep covenants made, we as Christians need to be aware that we are living in such an age and to heed Paul's admonition:

> But evil men and imposters will proceed from bad to worse, deceiving and being deceived. You, however, continue in the things you have learned and become convinced of, knowing from whom you have learned them (2 Timothy 3:13-14).

What became of Jim? The Spirit of God worked in his heart and after several sessions in which the sword of the Spirit was brought to bear on his conscience, he accepted biblical revelation rather than human rationalization. He confessed his impure desires, grew spiritually, and subsequently married the girl who had suggested the counseling.

Bob's story was a different one. No amount of evidence could dissuade him from his moral perversion, and he refused to respond to the Gospel. Lacking commitment, contract, and covenant in his relationship with his girlfriend, he soon left her and continued his self-centered pursuits, while she, disillusioned, turned to a lesbian relationship.

One study shows that one-third of couples who cohabit stay together an average of only four and one-half months; and further, authorities conclude that such men and women flounder from partner to partner in search of an ideal relationship.[8]

Clearly, this is not God's plan. He established marriage as a permanent covenant agreed upon by two people, presumably with the blessing of their parents. Marriage involves some form of an agreement, conformity to certain social customs, and consummation by physical union.

FOOTNOTES

1. "Sinfully Together," *Time,* July 9, 1979, p. 55.
2. Eleanor D. Macklin, "Going Very Steady," *Psychology Today,* November 1974, pp. 53-58.
3. Bill Heth, *Studia Theologica et Apologia,* "A Critique of the Evangelical Protestant View of Divorce and Remarriage," (P.O. Box 1030, Dallas, Texas, 1981), p. 14.
4. Abel Isaksson, *Marriage and Ministry in the New Temple,* Neil Tomkinson (trans.) with assistance of Jean Gray, (Lund: Gleerup; Copenhagen: Munksgaard, 1965), pp. 19-20.
5. Gordon Wenham, "The Marriage Bond and the Church," *Third Way,* (London, June 1978), p. 14; "May Divorced Christians Remarry?" *The Churchman,* Vol. 95, No. 2, p. 153, citing David Atkinson, *To Have and to Hold,* (London: Collins, 1979).
6. A.P. Ross, "Woman: In the Beginning," *Kindred Spirit,* Vol. 4, No. 4, Dallas Theological Seminary, Winter 1980, p. 10.
7. David Atkinson, *To Have and to Hold,* (Grand Rapids: Wm. B. Eerdmans Publishing Co., 1981), p. 70.
8. Nick Stinnett, *The Family and Alternative Lifestyles,* (Chicago: Nelson Hall, 1978), pp. 97, 100.

2

God's Purposes
for Marriage

The bride is wearing a white gown; the groom, a white tuxedo. The bridesmaids and groomsmen are dressed in coordinated colors, and the flowers are in place. The wedding party moves to the altar of the church as the organ plays. This is a wedding, one of the most beautiful and meaningful rituals the church practices. But where did it all originate? What are the underlying principles behind it?

To answer these questions we must go to the book of beginnings, the first book of the Old Testament. Its Hebrew title is taken from the first words of the book, "In the beginning," and the name in the English Bible, Genesis, comes from the Latin word for origin. Genesis is a book about the beginning of many things—the world, man, sin, civilization, the nations, and Israel. It also reveals the origins of human institutions and relationships.

Genesis 1 unfolds in brief but interesting detail the account of Creation, including the creation of the human race (male and female). In verses 26 to 30 we are given a clear picture of the uniqueness of mankind and the divine job description for the human couple. This picture is of fundamental importance to our understanding of the purposes God had for marriage.

Reflect the Image of God

Man was made in God's image:

> Then God said, "Let Us make man in Our image, according to Our likeness; . . . and God created man in His own image, in the image of God He created him; male and female. . . . Then the Lord God formed man of dust from the ground, and breathed into his nostrils the breath of life; and man became a living being (Genesis 1:26-27; 2:7).

Our understanding of marriage principles begins with the fact that God created man and woman distinct from all animal and plant life. Imprinted on man's very being is the image of God, so that man is a personal, rational, and moral being possessing intellect, emotion, and volition (Genesis 2:19-20; 3:6-7). The uniqueness of man gives him a special opportunity to fellowship with God and a special responsibility to obey His commands. It also provides him with the ability to relate on a deep level with his female counterpart.

The animal world, by contrast, operates on instinct, and mating is entirely intuitive. Animals do not have weddings, and one never speaks of the "marriage" of animals. Nor do we insist on monogamous or permanent relationships for them.

Human relationships are different. God established marriage and He insists on monogamous, heterosexual, and permanent relationships. Sin, of course, has distorted God's ideal, but God's immutable purposes remain the same, and man is never relieved of his moral responsibility as one made in the image of God (see Genesis 9:6; James 3:9).

Also significant is the fact that when Christ expounded on the permanence of marriage He pointed back to Genesis 1:27: "But from the beginning of creation, God made them male and female." (See Matthew 19:4 and Mark 10:6.) Clearly in the mind of Christ was man's obligation to embrace God's ideal. Why? Because man is created in God's image.

Help Rule the Earth

God gave mankind a stewardship with authority over all the earth. Psalm 8:4-8 speaks of this role: "What is man, that Thou dost take thought of him? . . . Thou hast made him a little lower than God. . . . Thou dost make him to rule over the works of Thy hands." Hebrews 2:5-10 reveals that sinful man's abortive attempt to fulfill this stewardship is ultimately restored in the redemptive work of Christ. The fact remains, however, that mankind still has a measure of sovereignty over creation. He is responsible to exercise that authority as a stewardship, under God's authority.

God established a husband-and-wife team as a way to carry out this responsibility. Tragically, it is often the tyranny of the material world, and man's failure to subdue it, that causes tension between the man and his wife. Because of sin, man struggles with his environment and often becomes its slave.

A divorce court judge in the state of New York who had presided over a record number of divorces was asked, "What do you think is the leading cause of divorce in our country today?" He replied without hesitation, "I think it is over whether one should squeeze the toothpaste tube in the middle or roll it up from the end." He then added, "What I mean is, little things like that cause tensions leading to marriage breakup."

It is incredible, isn't it, that man, with all of his skill, with his inventive genius, with his ability to split an atom and send a man to the moon, is still unable to fulfill his role as husband and father and maintain a productive family life.

It has been our observation during many years of ministry that a man or a woman who is capable of solving enormous problems in the business world, who is an expert at public relations, and who could be called a success by the world's standards, can find himself (or herself) inept at unraveling even the simplest problem that arises in the home, cannot get along with a mate, and can be a total failure in family life. Until man realizes that his stewardship over the earth begins by establishing a successful family life, and until he realizes that he can have that only as he submits to God's priorities, he is destined to fail.

Fill the Earth

A third purpose for marriage is to "be fruitful and multiply, and fill the earth" (Genesis 1:28). It was God's intention from the beginning that man and woman in their physical union be fruitful in the production of children. While we make no assumptions about the number of children a couple should have, it is clear that as modern man limits the size of his family for purely selfish or economic reasons, he is placing God's design for the home in jeopardy.

In 1945 most Americans felt that four or more children was the ideal; in 1980 two children was considered the maximum. During the past decade over ten million Americans chose sterilization, and the 1981 birthrate was 1.7, beneath the population replacement rate of 2.0. A poll taken by Yankelovich, Skelly, and White in 1981 showed that 83 percent of Americans now believe it is acceptable to marry and have no children. Incidentally, the same survey revealed that three out of four Americans consider being single and having children to be morally acceptable. This poll does not even mention the abortion epidemic that is sweeping across America. Social scientists pinpoint the reason for the declining birthrate: "We became obsessed with 'me' and making sure that we experienced it all."[1]

Psalm 127 tells us how God would build the home: "Behold, children are a gift of the Lord; the fruit of the womb is a reward. Like arrows in the hand of a warrior, so are the children of one's youth." This Scripture is not intended to dictate how many children one should have, but only to point out that one important purpose for marriage is to produce children.

When Malachi condemned the disruption of marriage, he said: "The Lord is acting as the witness between you and the wife of your youth, because you have broken faith with her, though she is your partner, the wife of your marriage covenant. Has not the Lord made them one? In flesh and spirit they are His. And why one? Because He was seeking godly offspring" (2:14-15, NIV).

God is the One who established unity in marriage. One reason He did is that He is seeking to raise up a godly seed. In a world where selfishness reigns, and more and more people are opting for fewer children, believers have a great motivation for being fruitful and multiplying, and filling the earth with a godly seed.

Provide Companionship

Genesis 2:18 and 20 state the fourth purpose for marriage—companionship. "Then the Lord God said, 'It is not good for the man to be alone' . . . but for Adam there was not found a helper suitable for him" (Genesis 2:18, 20).

It is God who first recognized that in spite of all the good things He had provided, man was still alone. God purposed to meet man's enormous need of companionship. He began by bringing every beast and bird to Adam and giving him the responsibility of naming them. As they passed in review before him, Adam made an amazing discovery. For all their infinite variety, there was none like him: "For Adam there was not found a helper suitable for him" (2:20). This condition of loneliness had been declared by God to be "not good" (2:18). Man needed someone to be his counterpart, someone to complement and complete him, someone to fill the areas where he was deficient. Man needed a companion.

The scriptural narrative uses a very important word to describe what was needed. Our English Bible translates this word "help meet" (KJV), or "helper suitable" (NASB; NIV). The Hebrew word employed in both verses 18 and 20 means "to surround, to protect." This word refers to a relationship where one supports, aids, or assists another. The same word is used in Psalm 46:1 where God is called "a very present help in trouble." This is the common word used for "help" or "helper," particularly in the psalms. In its numerous uses in the Old Testament, it implies that the one helped has some lack or deficiency. Most often it is used of the help which frail men need from the Lord (Genesis 49:25; Exodus 18:4; Deuteronomy 33:7).

Here in Genesis 2:20, however, it is speaking of the human assistance a wife can bring, fulfilling the husband's needs physically, spiritually, emotionally, and intellectually. She becomes his support, providing him with needed assistance; she is "suitable" for him, for she answers to his need. Where a husband is weak, a wife is often strong; where he lacks insight, she often possesses intuition. She has the capacity to meet his needs uniquely. The "helper" and the "helped" become partners in the joint venture of life. The role of helper is not one of servitude, but rather of significance and fulfillment. Even though the woman is the weaker vessel, she shares with her husband as a "fellow-heir of the grace of life" (1 Peter 3:7).

It should be observed that on occasion God calls a person to be single (1 Corinthians 7:25-26). This condition is to be neither despised nor scoffed at. It is apart from the norm but often necessary as a high calling from God so that one may concentrate his attention on service for Christ without distractions. In such cases God's grace compensates for the loneliness and other needs in a special way. But the norm is for a man and a woman to meet each other's needs within the context of marriage. In the Genesis account, the man had a need and God designed the woman to meet that need: "For indeed man was not created for the woman's sake, but woman for the man's sake" (1 Corinthians 11:9).

Man was formed or fashioned from the dust of the ground, but woman was made or built from Adam's side, "bone of my bones," and the surrounding "flesh of my flesh" (Genesis 2:23). God designed her and built her to careful specifications, making for Adam a perfect counterpart. Then God, as Father and Creator, brought her to the man (Genesis 2:22).

Some things should be carefully noted. First, God established heterosexual marriage. He did not provide Adam with another human being just like himself; the woman was created as his opposite. The words *man* and *woman* are different words. Certainly there was a difference mentally and emotionally, as well as physically. The two were to dovetail in every way.

Second, God established monogamous marriage. He gave Adam Eve, and no one else. Though polygamy is practiced in a sinful world, it is never the norm and always involves additional problems. God intended from the beginning that there be one man for one woman for life.

When God gave the woman to man, the need of his life was met. The words in Genesis 2:23 translated, "This is now" are much more expressive in the original language. It is an expression of excitement and fulfilled expectation roughly equivalent to our expression, "At last!" or "Eureka—I have found it!"

God set out to meet the need of Adam and meet it He did. Can you imagine the excitement of those moments as Adam and Eve began to discover how perfectly God had matched them? Man now had a companion. Malachi reminded Judah of this: "She is your companion and your wife by covenant" (2:14). Having a mate for companionship and to dispel one's loneliness is a legitimate purpose for marriage.

Enjoy a Covenant Partnership

In discovering the purposes of God in marriage, the bottom line is the covenant of marriage given in Genesis 2:24 and repeated by Christ and the Apostle Paul (Matthew 19:5; Mark 10:7-8; Ephesians 5:31). There is some dispute as to who spoke the words—Adam, God, or the author of the book, Moses. It seems logical to assume that the words constituted a kind of brief wedding pronouncement given by God Himself. Christ seemed to indicate this when He said, "He which made them at the beginning made them male and female, and said, 'For this cause' " (Matthew 19:4-5, KJV). Certainly the words are a part of the inspired text of both the Old and New Testaments and, there-fore, important to consider. The covenant involved three things: separation; unity and permanence; and intimacy.

1. Separation: "For this cause a man shall leave his father and mother. . . ."

Leaving one's parents indicates that one is to leave the deepest tie known to a child up to that time, in order to establish a new tie that actually supersedes the old. Parents nurture and care for a child. They train him and teach him by example and precept. They develop intimacy beyond expression, but their goal is to give the child both roots and wings—roots so he knows his heritage and has a sense of history and belonging, but wings because he will one day leave his parents for a relation-ship that has priority.

It can be assumed that if this, the closest of human ties, must be abandoned to establish a marriage, then all other lesser ties must also be severed. At the very outset of married life, the husband is to focus his full attention on meeting his wife's needs and the wife must likewise concentrate on meeting her hus-band's needs (1 Corinthians 7:32-34). Anything that would dis-tract from this priority must be set aside. In Israel when a man married, he was neither to go to war nor to be in charge of business for a full year so that he could concentrate his atten-tion on his new bride (Deuteronomy 24:5). All must be aban-doned so that the couple can build a real marriage with the kind of thrilling intimacy and interdependence that God intends in wedlock.

Some cautions, however, are needed. Leaving one's parents and friends does not mean shutting them out of your life. You should continue to honor your parents and value your friend-ships, but should not allow past ties to hinder the growth of your relationship with your mate.

Also, God never encourages a selfish or self-centered lifestyle. Whereas it is important to concentrate one's best efforts on each other, a couple should build spiritual values, ministry opportunities, and serve as a team together for the Lord. Failure to do this results in a lack of balance that eventually brings problems.

2. Unity and permanence: "... and shall cleave to his wife...."

You have probably seen a brand of glue called Permabond. On the label is a warning that this glue forms a permanent bond. It should be handled with care, therefore, because once sealed, objects glued together can never be parted without incurring severe damage. It would seem that modern marriage could use an application of Permabond. This concept is what God had in mind when He said that a man is to cleave to his wife. The word means "to cling to, to stick (or glue) to, to hold fast to someone in a permanent bond."

Cleaving as spoken of in Scripture is "clinging to someone in affection and loyalty." Man is to cleave to his wife (Genesis 2:24). Ruth clave to Naomi (Ruth 1:14). The men of Judah clave to David, their king, during Sheba's rebellion (2 Samuel 20:2). Shechem loved Dinah and clave to her (Genesis 34:3).[2]

Cleaving is an essential element in the covenant language of the Old Testament. "It is a technical term prominent in covenant terminology in Deuteronomy (10:20; 11:22; 13:4; 30:20; see also Joshua 22:5; 23:8)."[3] In those passages Israel is commanded to cleave to the Lord with intensity, to have a love that will not let go. This love may involve reverence and service, obedience, walking together, and love in action (Deuteronomy 10:20; 11:22; 13:4; 30:20). It is the same word used in Psalm 63:8 when the psalmist, in devotion to the Lord, says, "My soul followeth hard after Thee" (KJV), or "My soul clings to Thee" (NASB). Certainly the idea of cleaving is a wholehearted commitment to another in an inseparable union.

A man who cleaves to his wife will never give up; he will embrace her so closely that no wedge can ever come between them. He will utterly refuse any attitude or action that would allow friction to be created. He will "glue" himself to her in a permanent bond. When two people are married, God provides the glue and seals them in a union which is never to be broken.

When man tries to break that bond, the resulting damage is severe. Some analysts liken divorce to a suicide attempt in terms of the amount of stress that the person endures. It is no wonder that there are devastating effects when we try to "put asunder" what God has put together.

3. Intimacy: ". . . and they shall become one flesh."

Linked with the permanence of cleaving is the one-flesh concept that follows. Theologians have debated the meaning of one flesh. Some conclude that it refers only to the sexual relationship, while others have offered novel interpretations which have not been widely held in scholarly circles. The idea held by many scholars today is best expounded by Abel Isaksson[4] and mentioned by Gordon Wenham in his excellent commentary on Leviticus.[5]

It is a lengthy, detailed argument, but may be summarized as follows: Since to be "bone" and/or "flesh" of someone is a common term describing kinship,[6] the conclusion is that it is reasonable to translate "flesh" in Genesis 2:24 by the word "relation." Thus, the man leaves his "flesh" (his family) to establish a new family, creating vertical blood relations in the form of children and horizontal blood relationships between himself and his wife. This seems to be the best explanation of why God not only forbade marriages within literal (consanguinity) bloodlines (father/daughter, mother/son, brother/sister), but also forbade marriage to relations caused by another marriage (affinity, such as brother's wife, aunt by marriage, in-laws). Now all of this may sound complicated, but it seems to be the best explanation yet for the passage in Deuteronomy 24 where God does not allow the return of a woman to her first husband if there is a marriage in between.[7] Gordon Wenham adds:

> Through her first marriage the woman entered into the closest form of relationship with her husband. The patriarchal narratives suggest that it was regarded as quite proper to describe one's wife as one's sister (Genesis 12:13, 19; 20:2ff; 26:7ff). At any rate, divorce did not terminate this relationship; she still

counted as a very close relative. If a divorced couple want to come together again [after a second marriage], it would be as bad as a man marrying his sister. That is why it is described as "an abomination before the Lord" that causes "the land to sin" (Deuteronomy 24:4, KJV; see Jeremiah 3:1).[8]

These arguments indicate that marriage creates a remarkable intimacy and unity between families. (This consideration becomes very important in our discussion of the divorce and remarriage question in the later chapters of this book.) To be certain, "one flesh" implies the physical relationship between a man and wife, but it includes far more. In the words of A.P. Ross, "To become one flesh means becoming a spiritual, moral, intellectual, and physical unity."[9]

Thus the white gown and tuxedo, the flowers, the wedding party, all of these are only the trimmings of the wedding. The marriage between a man and woman is something that God established for creatures made in His image so that the husband and wife can better exercise their stewardship over the earth, produce children, and provide companionship for each other. They accomplish all these goals by entering into a covenant that involves leaving, cleaving, and becoming one flesh.

FOOTNOTES

1. Daniel Yankelovich, *New Rules: Searching for Self-Fulfillment in a World Turned Upside Down,* (Westminster, Md.: Random House, 1981).

2. R.L. Harris, G.L. Archer, Jr., and B.K. Waltke (eds.) *Theological Wordbook of the Old Testament,* Vol. 1, (Chicago: Moody Press, 1980), p. 178.
3. Bill Heth, *Studia Theologica et Apologia,* "A Critique of the Evangelical Protestant View of Divorce and Remarriage," (P.O. Box 1030, Dallas, Texas), p. 14.
4. Abel Isaksson, *Marriage and Ministry in the New Temple,* Neil Tomkinson (trans.) with assistance of Jean Gray; (Lund: Gleerup; Copenhagen: Munksgaard, 1965).
5. Gordon Wenham, *New International Commentary on the Old Testament, The Book of Leviticus,* (Grand Rapids: Wm. B. Eerdmans Publishing Co., 1979), p. 253.
6. Genesis 2:23; Genesis 29:12-14 (between uncle and nephew); Genesis 37:27 (between brothers); Judges 9:2 (between cousins); 2 Samuel 19:13 (between fellow tribesmen).
7. Bill Heth, *Studia Theologica et Apologia,* pp. 14-15.
8. Gordon Wenham, "The Restoration of Marriage Reconsidered," *Journal of Jewish Studies,* Vol, 30, 1979, p. 40.
9. A.P. Ross, "Woman: In the Beginning," *Kindred Spirit,* Vol. 4, No. 4, Dallas Theological Seminary, Winter 1980, p. 10.

3

Is Headship a Hardship?

Tom and Sue were in the office for premarital counseling. They had just finished an assignment from Ephesians 5 on the roles in marriage. When asked if they had any questions, tears of frustration welled up in Sue's eyes. "Does this mean I have to just do everything Tom says? I love him and I trust him a lot, but I can't stop being a person!"

Many women can identify with Sue's plight, and many men are equally confused about the proper balance in marriage.

Head/subordinate relationships are essential to any ordered society. Without clearly defined roles, a nation or community will give way to chaos and ultimate anarchy.

On every social strata, there can be productivity only as there is a harmonizing of roles. This harmony is especially important in the family. Dr. E.E. LeMasters in his book, *Parents in Modern America,*[1] said:

> In the modern American family male and female roles have been shifted and reorganized extensively since about 1920, and some families appear to be disorganized in *that nobody seems to know who is supposed to do what* (Italics ours).

Society may be confused, but God is not, and His unchange-able Word is clear. God the Creator assigns to husbands and wives roles that are intended to bring fulfillment and harmony.

When God created man and woman, He created "male and female" (Genesis 1:27), and their differences are many. He designed them so that each would fulfill a unique role and make a significant contribution to the other. The popular Dr. Joyce Brothers pointed out in *Woman's Day* [2] that there are dozens of differences between the male and female. She discussed items ranging from the difference in the angle at which the thigh is attached to the knee to differences in the brain.

Some today are pushing for a unisex culture where all distinc-tions between men and women (except in the sexual area) are broken down. That, quite simply, is impossible. God created Adam and Eve to complement each other; they are not identi-cal. The female skin is softer; the male blood is heavier; the male bones are larger and they are arranged differently. The male has 41 percent muscle as compared with a female's 35 percent. There are many significant differences.

It is not surprising then to discover in Scripture that God has given different assignments to the respective sexes. The Apos-tle Paul made clear that the leadership role in the church was to be assumed by the man because of his precedence in crea-tion: God made man first and woman second (1 Timothy 2:13). "Man was not created for the woman's sake, but woman for the man's sake" (1 Corinthians 11:9). God made a sovereign choice as to who was created first, and he fitted the man for the leadership role and the woman for the role as "a helper corre-sponding to" the man. It is safe to assume, therefore, that Adam was in charge in the Garden of Eden and Eve was fulfilled in her subordinate role.

Role Changes

The entrance of sin into the world brought about some dramatic changes. Adam was held responsible for the sin of the couple;

God addressed him specifically. "Then the Lord God called to the man and said to him, 'Where are you?' " When confronted by God, Adam tried to shift blame to Eve, but God held him responsible and thus death came to the human race through Adam (Genesis 3:9, 12; 1 Corinthians 15:22). Man was then driven from the Garden of Eden and the task of subduing the earth became toil (Genesis 3:17-19, 23-24).

Their roles were also drastically altered. The curse on Eve included not only the pain of childbearing but also a changed relationship with Adam: "Yet your desire shall be for your husband, and he shall rule over you" (Genesis 3:16). The word for desire used here has been variously interpreted. Some see it as sexual desire, while others see it as a desire for leadership or fulfillment. Actually, the word can mean "to long for," "to urge, to drive on, to impel," or "to control."

The angry Cain was told, "Sin is crouching at your door" and "desires to have you" (Genesis 4:7, NIV).[3] This phrase is the same as in Genesis 3:16. It is possible that the curse on the woman included a desire to rule over or dominate her husband. Born in a woman's heart is a rebellious and independent spirit that seeks "equality" and resists God-given authority.

Obviously, women are not alone in this tendency toward independence. Men too have insubordination in their hearts, but in this text God is addressing the issue of authority in the home. The Women's Liberation Movement did not originate in 1923 when the Equal Rights Amendment was first introduced in Congress, nor in 1966 when the National Organization for Women was founded. It was born in the heart of Eve because of sin.

Tension between men and women over their God-intended roles resulted from the Fall. Whereas the leadership of the husband and the willing submission of the wife were a matter of course in the original state, now the woman has a desire to dominate her leader. Hints of this conflict are seen in the Old Testament. Even godly women such as Sarah and Rebekah signaled their inward struggles by seeking to control and manipulate their mates (Genesis 16:2; 27:6-17). Women like Delilah (Judges 16) and Jezebel (1 Kings 21) are clear examples. Solomon spoke to the issue of the competing woman: "The contentions of a wife are a constant dripping" (Proverbs 19:13; see also Proverbs 21:9; 27:15; 25:24; 21:19). God never intended that a wife find her fulfillment in competing with her husband but in complementing him.

A Wife's Duty

In the New Testament, Paul and Peter both teach clearly about head/subordinate relationships in the family. The wife is to fulfill her duty to her husband (1 Corinthians 7:3). She is to give up her authority over her own body, and she is not to defraud her husband (7:4-5). She is to live to please her husband (7:34). She is to be subject to her husband as the church is subject to Christ; she is to reverence her husband (Ephesians 5:22, 24, 33). She is always to live in harmony with what is right (Colossians 3:18). Even if her husband is not obedient to God she is to obey him and quietly display by her behavior the attractiveness of a meek and quiet spirit (1 Peter 3:1-6).

The husband, on the other hand, is to fulfill his duty to his wife (1 Corinthians 7:3). He is to give up his authority over his own body and is not to defraud his wife (7:4-5). He is to live to please his wife (7:33). He is to love her with a self-sacrificing, unselfish love like Christ loved the church (Ephesians 5:25). He is to love her as his own body (5:28). He is not to be harsh with her (Colossians 3:19, NIV); he is to live with his wife in an understanding way, to honor her and to recognize that she is the weaker vessel, treating her as a fellow-heir of the grace of life (1 Peter 3:7).

These concepts do not imply that men are superior to women, nor do they allow for male domination. Quite the contrary. They admonish the wife to recognize that under proper authority she can be a productive and fulfilled person, making a unique and meaningful contribution in the marriage (Proverbs 31:10-31).

Her submission and obedience display a confident trust in God to work through constituted authority, even when the person holding that authority is out of step with God's Word (1 Peter 3:1, 5-6). It is not slavery; rather it is freedom to the highest degree. A wife's submission does not detract from her value as a person but contributes to making her a whole person, the person God intends for her to be.

Limited Authority

An additional word needs to be said to clarify the matter of submission to authority. We are a part of an evil world which is capable of great wrong. Because of that, the waters are often muddied as to what a person should do in specific cases. While the possible situations are too varied to deal with in detail here, some guidelines might be helpful.

All authority has limitations except for the authority of God. When a person in authority requires us to do something that is clearly forbidden by a higher authority, we are free to respectfully disobey.

Jane is a case in point. She came to me with a sad tale of a husband who was insisting on her being involved in a morally compromising situation with two other couples. Her question was obvious: "Do I have to submit to *that?*"

I answered with a question. "What does the Bible say about that kind of activity?"

She answered, "It expressly forbids it."

"So, what must you do?"

"Refuse?" she said hesitatingly.

"Yes, but why?"

"Because God's authority is greater than Fred's authority."

The apostles refused to obey the authority of the Sanhedrin for the same reason. "We must obey God rather than men" (Acts 5:29).

On the other hand, there must be real care in making certain that one has a definite direction from the higher authority before there is disobedience to the lesser.

When a woman becomes a Christian, she often is faced with a dilemma. Should she go with her husband on some outing on Sunday or go to church? The usual argument for disobeying the husband is Hebrews 10:25, "not forsaking our own assembling together."

Gerri is a good example of this kind of reasoning. When she came to me to get support for resisting her husband's wishes, she thought I would easily agree. After all, she had Scripture on her side. She was disappointed, however, because she had the misguided conception that the verse included, "at 11:00 on Sunday morning." When I asked if he had forbidden her to have *any* "assembling together" with other believers, she admitted that the problem was over Sunday morning and no other time. When she submitted on this point and enjoyed Christian fellowship and growth at other times more convenient for him, he soon became curious about her change of attitude and embraced her faith.

In dealing with hundreds of cases like these, I have suggested the following steps when it is clear that a husband's authority must be resisted.

• You must have so lived your life in submission to your husband that you can say in all honesty, "Darling, you know that I have never resisted you on anything, but now you are asking me to do something that is clearly forbidden." It does little good to appeal to Scripture as your defense if you have consistently been disobedient in other areas.

• Pray for a change. "The effective prayer of a righteous [woman] can accomplish much" (James 5:16).

• Be certain you understand the directive the husband has given. Don't assume you understand until you have clarified what he means, as well as what he says.

• Seek an alternative. Sometimes a husband has no idea how offensive certain activities may be to his wife. Try to discover what needs he is seeking to fulfill by that activity that might be met in a more legitimate way.

• Ask God for wisdom in confronting your husband in a Christ-like manner. Don't forget the meek and quiet spirit of 1 Peter 3:4.

• Maintain a godly attitude. Read again 1 Peter 2:18-25 and keep that in mind as you consider the word "likewise" in 1 Peter 3:1.

• Maintain an attitude of submission in all other areas of the relationship. A major problem that arises in cases like these is that the wife loses respect for the husband and conveys the idea that since he made the mistake she does not have to obey at all.

• Make a carefully worded appeal to the husband with a cheerful, positive attitude mingled with words that assure him of your genuine concern for his welfare and your continued, undiminished love.

• If he insists, explain why you cannot obey. The Scripture is clear that no Christian wife should do anything contrary to civil law or in violation of Scripture. In the case of such things as child abuse, stealing, lying, or immorality, the wife should obey the law and obey God rather than man.

• Be willing to suffer the consequences for obedience to God.

Maude had not been a Christian very long when she cheerfully announced that she was going to divorce her husband. When she sensed I did not share her enthusiasm she asked, "Why?" Her husband was not a believer, an alcoholic, sometimes abusive, and failing to meet her needs in any way. He often insisted she do things she did not want to do and she was "fed up." She had expected the support of her pastor, but she was in for a surprise. Together we evaluated each request and discovered that though some were unreasonable, not one was forbidden by God. That was ten years ago. The husband is still not a believer, but has begun to come to church, and the children have grown in the Lord. Maude said to me the other day that the joy of serving the Lord by loving her husband and submitting to him has been overwhelming. There have been times when she has had to use the steps previously suggested, but in each case God has accomplished growth in her life and an eventual easing of the situation.

A Husband's Duty

While God requires submission on the part of the wife, He never intended that the husband be a dictator or a despot over her. The picture of the husband as a leader is that of a loving, caring, benevolent manager. He is to be the leader/servant that Christ portrayed in Matthew 20:25-28. In the text Christ defined the pagan model of leadership as being either dominant dictatorship—"You know that the rulers of the Gentiles lord it over them"—or charismatic control—"And their great men exercise authority over them, but it shall not be so among you" (Matthew 20:25-26). True biblical leadership is a serving leadership.

> Whoever wishes to become great among you shall be your servant, and whoever wishes to become first among you shall be your slave; just as the son of Man did not come to be served, but to serve, and to give His life a ransom for many (Matthew 20: 26-28).

Paul applied this concept directly in writing to the Ephesian church when he pointed out that the nature of a husband's love should be akin to Christ's love for the church. That love led to sacrifice (Ephesians 5:25, "gave"), setting the church apart for sacred use (5:26, "sanctify"), a desire for its purity (5:26, "cleanse"), and a desire to present to Himself a perfect bride (5:27). Paul became intensely personal when he further related the relationship to the way a man cares for his own body. A husband is to nourish and cherish his wife for she is a part of his own body. The lifelong goal of every husband should be to so serve his wife that she will be freed to attain her maximum potential as his helper.

There are differences between a man and a woman, physically, mentally, emotionally, and God intends that the man and woman fulfill different roles. Reversing those roles or ignoring them can cause great stress on a marriage and create tensions that threaten to destroy the harmony God intends in the marriage bond.

Attacks on Traditional Roles

These traditional roles are very much under attack today. The National Organization of Women is seeking to overthrow what it calls "antifeminist roles." The United Church of Christ is attempting to drop the sexism phrases in its official language so that "brethren in Christ" becomes "kindred in Christ," "mankind" is changed to "humankind," "chairman" is altered to "chairperson," "sons of God" becomes "children of God," and "he" becomes "he or she."

One churchwomen's organization protested to the church leadership about the use of Colossians 3 in the services because Paul admonishes wives to submit to their husbands and the accompanying footnote says: "Paul outlines ideal family relationships." The women said that the reading is antifeminist and unrealistic in modern times. They suggested the mutual love exhortations of 1 John 4 as a substitute.

Another married couple—both ordained Presbyterian ministers — tried to work out egalitarian roles by joining their last names with a hyphen, sharing one position as "associate minister" of a church, each being on the job half the time, each getting half the pay, and each doing half the housework.

Such examples are symptoms of a much deeper problem—people's rebellion against the plan and purpose of God.

God's Plan

Esther and George had agreed when they were married to be equals in their relationship, but were now facing the utter failure of their marriage. When they finally came for counsel, their marriage was, in their words, "hopeless." When I suggested that they try it God's way, they were shocked that anyone could hold such a "medieval idea" as wives submitting and husbands leading. I pointed out that their way was a failure—why not give God's way a chance? The process was painful and success was not immediately obtained; but with God's help, Esther began to yield to George and George falteringly began to lead. It was about four years later that Esther shared that she was "the most fulfilled woman in the world." She said, "I never dreamed I could be happy under my husband's authority, but until I submitted to him I did not even know what being a woman was all about."

After Miltinnie and her husband came to the Lord, she was confronted with the biblical teaching on submission.

"When I first heard that the Bible taught a wife should submit to her husband, my initial response was unbelief. God would not do that to me! After looking up the reference, I decided that perhaps it was not something for today. After all, times have changed."

Even though she tried to suppress the truth, it kept gnawing at her. Finally, she submitted to the Lord. "I admitted that I had all along tried to change my husband and had never once thought that I might be the one who needed to change." That change brought with it the acknowledgment and confessions of other behaviors as sin. And this in turn helped her build a strong and solid relationship in the marriage.

"Marriage," she writes, "has to be lived out within the context of its Creator, His plan and purpose for it. It can be a 'hellacious' torment or a heavenbound joy. The choice is to reject or accept God's plan. I, for one, have not regretted saying, 'I do' to God."[4]

God's way is always superior to man's futile attempts at substitutes.

Let the wicked forsake his way,
And the unrighteous man his thoughts;
And let him return to the Lord,
And He will have compassion on him;
And to our God,
For He will abundantly pardon.
"For My thoughts are not your thoughts,
Neither are your ways My ways," declares the Lord.
"For as the heavens are higher than the earth,
So are My ways higher than your ways,
And My thoughts than your thoughts." (Isaiah 55:7-9).

FOOTNOTES

1. E.E. LeMasters, *Parents in Modern America,* (Homewood, Ill.: The Dorsey Press, 1970), p. 51.
2. Joyce Brothers, "Men & Women—The Differences," *Woman's Day,* February 9, 1982, p. 58.
3. Susan T. Foh, *Women and the Word of God,* (Nutley, N.J.: Presbyterian & Reformed Publishing Co., 1980), pp. 67-69.
4. Miltinnie Yih, "A Redeemed Marriage," *Challenger,* June 1982, pp. 2-3.

4

Christ, A Man's Example

In our age of independence and anarchy, there are great misunderstandings as to what constitutes head/subordinate relationships. One radical feminist said, "Since marriage constitutes slavery for women, it is clear that the women's movement must concentrate on attacking this institution. Freedom for women cannot be won without the abolition of marriage."[1]

What is it that gives people such an impression of the roles in marriage? Part of the misunderstanding comes from wrong practice on the part of many married people. Husbands often misunderstand their role and dominate rather than serve. They feel their duty is to bring their wives into subjection, like a cowboy breaks a bronco, rather than tenderly caring for their wives and loving them gently into submission. The husband who continually says, "I'm in charge here!" is really not in charge. In Scripture there are models of ideal headship and subordination, and both are found in our Lord Jesus Christ. In 1 Corinthians 11:3 we read, "Christ is the head of every man" (ideal headship), and "God is the head of Christ" (ideal subordination). As the Son of God, Christ is coeternal and coequal with the Father. As the Son of man, He is perfect man in total subjection to the Father and with total authority over His disciples. Thus we can watch His life unfold in the Gospels and see practical examples for any head/subordinate relationship and, in particular, the husband/wife relationship.

Christ as Subordinate

1. He gave up His rights. An essential element in any subordinate role is that of surrendering one's rights. When Christ healed a man on the Sabbath and was challenged by the Pharisees, He answered, "My Father is working until now, and I Myself am working" (John 5:17). This reply irritated the Jews, who rightly understood it to mean that He was claiming equality with God. Jesus did not deny their accusation, but answered, "The Son can do nothing of Himself, unless it is something He sees the Father doing; for whatever the Father does, these things the Son also does in like manner" (John 5:19).

Here is a picture of ideal subordination. Jesus Christ gave up His rights. Paul refers to Christ's "self-emptying" in Philippians 2:5-8. Can you imagine the harmony that could come to a home if the wife were willing to surrender all her rights to her husband? If she were willing to give up her right to privacy, her right to spend money as she sees fit, her right to freedom, and her right to selfish thoughts? What a difference such a surrender would make in the home!

2. His objective was always the glory of His Head. Christ knew that because of His union with the Father, whenever the Father was glorified He shared in that glory. In John 13, when the scene was set for the crucifixion by the departure of Judas, Christ said, "Now is the Son of Man glorified, and God is glorified in Him; if God is glorified in Him, God will also glorify Him in Himself, and will glorify Him immediately" (John 13:31-32).

Paul pointed out that man "is the image and glory of God; but the woman is the glory of man" (1 Corinthians 11:7). Vine suggests that this means that the woman renders "conspicuous the authority of the man."[2] A wife should so conduct herself to make her husband's headship obvious. She must be committed to making her mate a successful husband and father. Like the special wife of Proverbs 31, "She does him good and not evil all the days of her life" (v. 12).

3. He trusted His Head implicitly even when all was against Him. Christ's words on the cross were, "Father, into Thy hands I commit My spirit" (Luke 23:46). The word *commit* means "to place alongside"; it has the sense of depositing something with another for safekeeping, or entrusting to.

A different word used in 1 Peter 2:23 conveys the idea even more strongly: Christ "kept entrusting Himself to Him who judges righteously." That trust enabled Him to refrain from reviling or threatening or committing sin or deceit, even when He was abused and mocked and crucified.

It is important to note that it is in this context we read, "In the same way, you wives, be submissive to your own husbands" and, "In this way in former times the holy women also, who hoped in God, used to adorn themselves, being submissive to their own husbands" (1 Peter 3:1, 5). Implicit trust in one's head is a mark of godliness and Christian maturity.

4. Christ did not please Himself but lived to please His Head. His was the way of self-denial. "For even Christ pleased not Himself" (Romans 15:3, KJV). Thus, the Father could say, both at Christ's baptism and at His transfiguration, "This is My beloved Son, in whom I am well-pleased" (Matthew 3:17; see also Matthew 17:5; Mark 1:11; Luke 3:22; 2 Peter 1:17). Every breath He drew, every word He spoke, every deed He accomplished was designed to do one thing—please the One who was His Head. Is it any wonder that Paul uses this illustration in Romans 15 to tell believers that we are "not to please ourselves." Then he adds, "Let every one of us please his neighbor for his good to edification" (Romans 15:1-2, KJV).

While this is true for all Christians, it may be applied specifically to wives under the authority of their husbands. A faithful wife will seek to edify her husband; she will live to please him. "One who is married is concerned about the things of the world, how she may please her husband" (1 Corinthians 7:34).

5. Christ was totally resigned to the will of His Father's authority. Even in His most trying hour, Christ's attitude was, "Not My will, but Thine be done" (Luke 22:42). Facing the cross, He said to Peter, "The cup which the Father has given Me, shall I not drink it?" (John 18:11)

The psalmist said of Him, "I delight to do Thy will, O my God" (Psalm 40:8, KJV; see also Hebrews 10:7, 9). In His pattern prayer, Jesus said, "Thy will be done, on earth as it is in heaven" (Matthew 6:10). In the Bread of Life passage in John's Gospel, Christ declared, "For I have come down from heaven, not to do My own will, but the will of Him who sent Me" (John 6:38). Earlier He had said, "I can do nothing on My own initiative. As I hear, I judge; and My judgment is just, because I do not seek My own will, but the will of Him who sent Me" (John 5:30). When Christ was in Samaria He told His disciples, "My food is to do the will of Him who sent Me, and to accomplish His work" (John 4:34).

There is no doubt that much marriage conflict is a result of a battle of wills. Such conflict is short-circuited, however, when a wife resigns herself to the will of her husband, her head. A subordinate role is never easy, but it can be fulfilling and bring joy and harmony when one is yielded to God and thereby submissive to all authority.

Christ as Head

1. Christ maintained the heart of a servant. He never denied that He was the Master, yet He stooped to wash the disciples' feet. Then He said, "You call Me Teacher and Lord; and you are right; for so I am. If I then, the Lord and the Teacher, washed your feet, you also ought to wash one another's feet" (John 13:13-14). As a leader He knew what it was to serve others by love (Galatians 5:13). He characterized His own

ministry this way: "For even the Son of Man did not come to be served, but to serve, and to give His life a ransom for many" (Mark 10:45).

The world desperately needs husbands who are infected with this attitude of servanthood. A woman will respond to a man who can stoop, who can bend, and who can demonstrate the heart of a servant.

2. Christ demonstrated self-sacrificing love. John said of Christ as He surveyed the disciples in the upper room, "Having loved His own who were in the world, He loved them to the end" (John 13:1). Christ said, "Greater love has no one than this, that one lay down his life for his friends" (John 15:13). His was a love that took Him to a Roman cross. He laid down His life for the sheep (John 10:11). He loved us and gave Himself for us (Galatians 2:20, KJV). John said it this way:

> We know love by this, that He laid down His life for us; and we ought to lay down our lives for the brethren. . . . Little children, let us not love with word or with tongue, but in deed and truth (1 John 3:16, 18).

Our society is not accustomed to sacrifice, but the Christian life is one of denying oneself and taking up a cross and following Jesus Christ (Mark 8:34). This attitude of self-denial and sacrifice is essential for a husband, especially since he is commanded to love his wife "just as Christ also loved the church and gave Himself up for her" (Ephesians 5:25).

3. Christ empathized with the weakness of those under Him. The foolishness, impulsiveness, and failure of the disciples are evident throughout the Gospels. But evident as well are Christ's patience, His kindness, and His tenderness. Even when He needed to rebuke, He displayed love and understanding. Today He sympathizes with our weaknesses and when we are faithless, He remains faithful (Hebrews 4:15; 2 Timothy 2:13).

Even if a man finds it difficult to understand how his wife feels and thinks, he is still expected to live with her "in an under-standing way, as with a weaker vessel, since she is a woman" (1 Peter 3:7). It is a special kind of man who can identify with his wife in her weakness and need, but Christ makes such understanding possible.

4. Christ assumed responsibility for His disciples, meeting their needs and preparing for their future. When Christ saw His men foundering on the sea, He rescued them and calmed them with words of assurance: "It is I; do not be afraid" (John 6:20). During the three years He was with them, He provided them with food, took care of their taxes, prepared a place for their future, and provided a Comforter for them in their present circumstances (Mark 8:4-9; Matthew 17:27; John 14:2, 16). He prayed for them; and when He was taken by the temple guard, He offered Himself and urged the soldiers to release His follow-ers (John 17; 18:8). Christ saw those under His authority as a sacred trust "given" to Him by God and He demonstrated genuine concern for them (John 17:6; 10:29).

But the greatest contribution Christ made to His disciples was a spiritual one. Wherever they went, whatever they did as a "family," the Head was always feeding His followers with spiritual truth. He used the lilies of the field and the sparrows to remind them of God's care, and a sower planting a crop to teach about spiritual growth. He aroused His disciples' curiosity with parables, and He took them with Him into the world of the miraculous. Asking questions to make them think, He constant-ly called for commitment on their part. He was their spiritual leader par excellence. He showed them how to forgive as He forgave the paralytic man and the adulterous woman (Mark 2:9; John 8:3-11). When He hung on a Roman cross between two thieves, He cried out, "Father, forgive them; for they do not know what they are doing" (Luke 23:34).

Christ taught His disciples to love one another, to love their neighbors, and even to love their enemies (John 15:12; Mat-thew 19:19; 22:39; Mark 12:31, 33; Luke 10:27; Matthew

5:44; Luke 6:27, 35). He then exemplified that love by loving the rich young ruler (Mark 10:21), caring for disciples (John 14:21; 15:9), and showing compassion to the multitudes (Matthew 9:36; 14:14; 15:32; Mark 6:34; 8:2), to the sick (Matthew 20:34; Mark 1:41), to the needy (Luke 7:13), and the demon-possessed (Mark 5:19). The greatest demonstration of love in human history was Christ giving His life for sinners (1 John 3:16; Romans 5:10).

Husbands become very adept at "telling" their wives what to do, but too often it stops there. Men ought to gently guide their wives by their own example, just as Christ did for His disciples.

Because this same Christ indwells each Christian, it is gloriously possible to exemplify His character, in the power of the Holy Spirit.

A wise man once said, "Ideals are like stars; we will not succeed in touching them with our hands; but following them as the seafaring man on the desert of waters, we will reach our destiny." Christ presents the ideal in head/subordinate relationships. If we follow Him, we will reach our goal.

FOOTNOTES

1. Margaret M. Paloma and T. Neal Garland, "The Married Professional Woman: A Study in the Tolerance of Domestication," *Journal of Marriage and the Family,* August 1971, p. 533 (quoting Shelia Cronan).
2. W.E. Vine, *Vine's Expository Dictionary of New Testament Words,* Vol. 2, (Old Tappan, N. J.: Fleming H. Revell Co., 1966), p. 154.

5

Keys to Harmony

Someone has said, "Marriages don't fail. People fail. Broken marriage is just a casualty."[1]

God has given us His Word to transform us, and with transformation comes the potential of reconciliation and restoration of even the most severely broken relationships. The Bible says a great deal about relationships. The more than twenty-four "one another" concepts—forbearing one another, admonishing one another, forgiving one another, being kind to one another (Ephesians 4:2; Romans 15:14; Ephesians 4:32), as well as the "oughts" of Scripture—you ought to bear the infirmities of the weak, you ought to love one another (Romans 15:1; 1 John 4:11), show that God is seeking to remake and remold relationships to a divine ideal.

First Peter 3:8-12 gives important and helpful guidelines for bringing new vitality to any relationship, especially marriage. In the preceding verses Peter emphasized the responsibility of the wife to win her unbelieving husband by a meek and quiet spirit (1 Peter 3:1-6), and the responsibility of the husband to live with his wife in an understanding way (1 Peter 3:7). Then he summarized by saying, "To sum up, let all be harmonious, sympathetic, brotherly, kindhearted, and humble in spirit" (v. 8). Because each of these five words gives an insight into proper relationships, they have special application to the close husband/wife relationship.

Harmony

The Greek word for harmony literally means "same mind." Thus harmony is produced by having the same mind. This particular word for mind, however, includes the idea of having a certain mind-set (as also in Colossians 3:2 and Romans 8:6).

Now the particular mind-set that our text refers to should be the same for both the husband and the wife. Does this mean they will always agree? Of course not. Remember that the husband and wife complement each other. There will be differences of opinion. A life that is "just plain vanilla" is very bland, and a monotone who sings the same note repeatedly is boring. God put great variety into His world, and the contrasts and differences make His created world exciting. The same thing is true of relationships. Not only are males and females different in many ways, but each individual personality has its own color and flavor.

Harmony is defined as "pleasing or congruent arrangements of parts or sounds."[2] It implies complementing parts or sounds which complete the whole. Harmony in marriage is not total agreement on every point, but rather a concord that comes by each one making his unique contribution to the whole so that the "chord" is complete. In music a chord can have a dissonant note which sounds harsh for a moment, but being resolved adds color and welcome variety to the whole piece. In a marriage relationship, there may be a time when a question is unresolved. It seems harsh and tense and then one little adjustment is made and there comes a recognition not only of the prevailing harmony but also of the purpose for the sour note as well.

A marriage should be a symphony of two persons in accord with one another. There is no room for one to sing a solo or to do his or her own arrangement, since the two individuals should be blended in perfect harmony. Nor is there a place for a false crescendo of deceit, nor an untrue note because one's life is "off pitch." The husband and wife should be in touch with God and each other and offer a glorious paean of praise that will delight the heart of God. The mind-set of a husband and wife should be to resolve all disputes so that there is eventual harmony.

Sympathy

Akin to the idea of harmony is the concept of sympathy. The original word is *sumpatheō,* which means "to suffer with." This verb is used in Hebrews 4:15, which the KJV renders "touched with" and the NASB translates "sympathize." The word suggests being touched with the other person's feelings, identifying with a person in his pain and sorrow, weeping when the other person weeps and rejoicing when he rejoices (Romans 12:15). Sympathy and selfishness cannot coexist. As long as self is the most important thing in the world, true sympathy cannot be present.

Sympathy is a willingness to step out of self, out of one's own wants and desires, and identify totally with the hurt, pain, and sorrow, as well as the joy and success of the other person.

Christ identified totally with mankind and was "touched with the feeling of our infirmities" (Hebrews 4:15, KJV). In the church there is to be unity. For that reason when one part of the body suffers the other part sympathizes. In 1 Corinthians 12:25-26 we read, "The members should have the same care for one another. And if one member suffers, all the members suffer with it; if one member is honored, all the members rejoice with it."

If this is to be true of the Christian body, it should also be characteristic of the husband/wife relationship which illustrates the church (Ephesians 5:23-24). Since a man and wife are "one flesh" (5:31), when one part of that flesh is hurting the other part should empathize. When two people in a relationship are focusing unselfishly on each other's needs, there is always a sweet and sympathetic spirit.

Brotherliness

It may seem strange to speak of "brotherliness" in terms of the marriage relationship, but it is only because we lack understanding of the Greek concept of brotherly love. The original word *philadelphoi* is carried over into English in the word Philadelphia (brotherly love). This comes from the words *philos* (close friends) and *adelphos* (near kinsman).

The word *adelphos* is used in the New Testament for kinship in the Christian community, without regard to sexual distinction. It speaks of those with common interests and pursuits, who are united by a common calling, as brothers (Revelation 22:9). It suggests a relationship based on common origin and life. Certainly a man and wife share a kinship and life that is beyond any other human relationship.

The word *philos* is even richer in its implications. It is the Greek word for a deep abiding friendship. Aristotle emphasized the extent of this relationship when he said, "The things of close friends (plural of *philos*) are jointly owned," and "A man's close friend (*philos*) is another himself."

In Aristotle's first statement, the idea is of a relationship so close that neither person thinks of his property as "mine" but rather as "ours." God intends that a man and wife have this kind of relationship. Even one's body no longer belongs to himself, but is given over to the authority of his partner (1 Corinthians 7:4). Dangers abound in marriages in which this concept is not followed. Wives often have money or furniture they call "mine." Husbands may have money, cars, or boats they call "mine." God intends that in the marriage all things are "ours." When two people are united in a common interest and purpose to share their life together (and all that implies), they can be said to be "brotherly."

Aristotle's second statement pinpoints the meaning of the

various forms of *philos* in the New Testament. "A man's close friend is another himself" pictures friendship that is so intimate, so compatible, so all-embracing, that even if one party is absent for the moment, the other party can accurately reflect his response. Perhaps that is why Jesus chose to use the word *philos* instead of the more common *agapé* when He said in John 5:20, "For the Father loves [*phileo*] the Son, and shows Him all things that He Himself is doing." It also could explain why the disciples and the Jews used this word in speaking of the relationship between Lazarus and Jesus (John 11:3, 36) and why John, the beloved disciple, referred to himself as the *philos* of Jesus (John 20:2).

Inherent in the word *philos* is the idea of the closest tie of friendship and compatibility. Two people in a *philos* relationship like the same things, enjoy mutual interests, and learn to share new experiences together. Fellowship, close companionship, and camaraderie are parts of a *philos* relationship. A husband and wife should be sharing thoughts and feelings, plans and dreams, hopes and aspirations. The Old Testament prophet asked, "Can two walk together, except they be agreed?" (Amos 3:3, KJV) The obvious answer is No! A couple must "agree to agree" on basic things and learn to enjoy each other's likes. Compatibility requires a lot of adjustment and adaptation on the part of both the husband and the wife. But it can be done, and results are delightful.

Kindheartedness
In the closing scene of the classic novel, *Gone with the Wind,* Rhett Butler tells Scarlett O'Hara that he just does not care anymore. His indifference is dressed in emphatic language that has a curt finality to it. It fairly represents the attitude of thousands of married individuals today. But God commands that Christians do care.

The Greek word translated "kindhearted" is also made up of two parts, a prefix which generally means "well" and a word that refers to the digestive tract. The word in its pure form simply refers to the entrails or the innards of a man or an animal. The ancient Greeks thought of emotion as being related to the bowels rather than the heart, so this word came to mean "the strongest feeling of a merciful (Matthew 18:27) or loving (Luke 15:20) reaction."[3] Thus the word is used to convey the idea of compassion we associate with the heart today. In fact, the same root is used eight times in the Gospels to speak of Christ's compassion (Matthew 9:36; 14:14; 15:32; 20:34; Mark 1:41; 6:34; 8:2; Luke 7:13). It is consistently translated "felt compassion" or was "moved with compassion." W.E. Vine suggests the rendering, "to be moved as to one's inwards."[4]

There obviously is a close relationship between compassion and sympathy. Sympathy is "to feel with"; compassion is "to feel for." Sympathy causes one to feel as another feels; compassion leads to constructive action. It is a love and affection that grips and profoundly moves the whole man. There is not a faltering marriage in the world that would not improve dramatically if both parties began to have this deep caring concern for each other.

During recent years we have become so accustomed to hearing dramatic news reports of tragedy and human distress that we have lost our ability to care. Hardness of heart has become characteristic of our age. Christ blamed hardness of heart for the Mosaic divorce legislation (Matthew 19:8). It was hardness of heart that caused the Israelites to err; and it is hardness of heart that keeps people from repentance, brings destruction, and causes people to fall into calamity (Psalm 95:8; Romans 2:5; Proverbs 29:1; 28:14).

Paul spoke of those who were ignorant "because of the hardness of their heart" and then pointed out that they had "become callous" or, as the *Authorized Version* has it, "past feeling," (Ephesians 4:18-19, KJV). It was in this setting that Paul called for Christians to be different.

But you did not learn Christ in this way. . . . Be renewed in the spirit of your mind. . . . Let all bitterness and wrath and anger and clamor and slander be put away from you, along with all malice. And be kind to one another, tenderhearted [same words as in our text], forgiving each other, just as God in Christ also has forgiven you (Ephesians 4:20, 23, 31-32).

Because of calloused hearts, people just close their eyes to problems and hope they go away. Even though they would rather escape from problems than face them and compassionately solve them, God does not give Christians that option. He joins a man and a woman in an inseparable union and then commands them to have a mutual care for one another.

Humility

The last of these important words is the common word for humility. Many people have strange ideas about what constitutes humility. Some believe it means to "grovel in the dust," to "efface oneself," or to reduce one's self-image to shambles. This is not humility. Trying to act humble is not humility.

Peter used the common Greek word for humble, together with the word we saw earlier in this chapter for mind or mindset. The Greeks often used their word for humility to describe a river that was running low. Bishop Richard Trench points out that humility is a right and proper estimate of oneself, and he quotes St. Bernard's definition, "The esteeming of ourselves small, inasmuch as we are so; the thinking truly, and because truly, therefore, lowly, of ourselves."[5]

Trench goes on to point out that the key to understanding humility is a mind-set "of absolute dependence, of having nothing, but receiving all things of God."[6] A study of pride and humility in the Old and New Testaments underlines this emphasis. If we consider the more than one hundred times the word *proud* or *pride* is used in Scripture and the more than seventy times the word *humble* or *humility* is used, we can see that there is a common denominator in each text. Pride always is speaking of one who is independent; humility refers to one who realizes that he is *dependent.* That is why "God is opposed to the proud, but gives grace to the humble" (1 Peter 5:5).

Pride and humility are used in the Bible primarily to speak of our relationship with God. Whether we are living independent of God or dependent upon God will reflect in our relationships with others. Thus when we are told to be humble with others (Romans 12:16; 1 Peter 5:5), in essence we are urged to realize that we have no reason for distinction in God's eyes because we are all dependent creatures. We should also realize that we are dependent upon each other. Paul pointed out that all the members of the church are dependent on the Head, Christ, and that there is also an interdependence on each other (1 Corinthians 12:12-27). Therefore, we need to recognize the function and contribution of each part and exercise a mutual care one for the other.

When Peter called on the husband and the wife to be "humble in spirit," he seemed to be urging them to live in dependence upon God and to realize an interdependence on each other.

This is in the spirit of Ecclesiastes 4:9-10, "Two are better than one because they have a good return for their labor. For if either of them falls, the one will lift up his companion. But woe to the one who falls when there is not another to lift him up."

It is interesting to notice how we treat others differently when they really need us. A man and a wife should realize that they are made one and, therefore, are incomplete without the other. An attitude of independence does not belong in marriage. Husbands and wives need to say often, "I need you."

Harmony, sympathy, brotherly love, compassion, and humility—five basic attitudes that can bring new vitality to a marriage relationship. One other thing must be added, however. In 1 Peter 3:9 we read, "Not returning evil for evil, or insult for insult, but giving a blessing instead; for you were called for the very purpose that you might inherit a blessing." Perhaps the biggest roadblock that bars people from enjoying the fruit of these five attitudes is the penchant man has for revenge, for wanting to even the score. Satan has sold us the false doctrine that if someone hurts us we will lose out if we do not retaliate.

Just recently a woman came to me and said, "When my husband changes, I will change, but not before." That kind of an attitude can only produce a stalemate. She had been matching insult for insult and returning evil for evil for two years, and the marriage was fast deteriorating. What could be done? I suggested she make a list of all of her husband's positive qualities. After a struggle she did, and much to her surprise she had seventeen things on her list. Then I asked her to do two things with that list. First, thank God for each of those qualities. Second, praise her husband for at least one of those qualities each day.

Finally, I explained the five attitudes of 1 Peter 3:8-12, and urged her to begin to develop them in her life. She purposed to do this. The very next day when her husband was being very unreasonable, she took his side and harmonized with his demands. She tried to empathize and care. As she analyzed his request, she actually found that what he wanted was pleasing to her as she adjusted to it. The husband calmed down when he saw she was not going to resist, and then she praised him for his firm leadership and asked his forgiveness for her rebellious attitudes. Within a week that man was in my office, confessing his sins and seeking God's forgiveness.

Results are not always that dramatic. However, application of these attitudes does work and will prove effective if given enough time, since this is what God prescribes.

Let him who means to love life and see good days refrain his tongue from evil and his lips from speaking guile. And let him turn away from evil and do good; let him seek peace and pursue it. For the eyes of the Lord are upon the righteous, and His ears attend to their prayer, but the face of the Lord is against those who do evil (1 Peter 3:10-12).

FOOTNOTES

1. Source unknown.
2. *Webster's New Collegiate Dictionary,* (G. & C. Merriam Co., 1977).
3. H.H. Lesser, *The New International Dictionary of New Theology,* Vol. 2, Colin Brown, ed., (Grand Rapids: Zondervan Publishing Co., 1978), pp. 599-600.
4. W.E. Vine, *Expository Dictionary of New Testament Words,* (Old Tappan, N. J.: Fleming H. Revell Co., 1966), p. 218.
5. Richard Chevenix Trench, *Synonyms of the New Testament,* (Grand Rapids: Wm. B. Eerdmans Publishing Co., 1953), pp. 140-141.
6. Ibid.

6

What's Forever For?

A currently popular song asks the questions, "Doesn't anybody stay together any more?" and "If love doesn't last forever, then what's forever for?"[1]

The song seems to indicate an increasing cynicism on the part of young people today about the future of marriage as we know it. Unfortunately, many people do not see the instability in relationships.

Prominent Hollywood personality Neile Adams was divorced from actor Steve McQueen in 1971. She stated, "Steve and I now realize it is impossible to love one person for your entire life."[2]

Many Americans subscribe to this blasé attitude. Marriages are being sealed with little or no thought to lifelong commitment. "Till death do us part" has become "Till divorce do us part." The 1980s face a new dilemma—the children of the divorce generation are now getting married and their only knowledge of marriage is from a series of broken homes around them. Currently, there are more than eleven million children under the age of eighteen whose parents are divorced, and it is estimated that one million more children per year will suffer through the dissolution of their families.[3]

The child from a broken home may enter marriage with serious doubts as to whether it is possible for a marriage to endure the pressures of modern society.

Add to this the fact that "the divorce rate in remarriage families is approximately ten percent higher than in first marriages"[4]—some claim it is still higher—and you increase the scope of the problem considerably.

The *Chicago Tribune* printed a divorce guide the week of November 8, 1981 in its Tempo section. The lead article focused on "some constructive ideas on dismantling a marriage." It reported, "For every two weddings in America last May, one couple divorced." Reporter Laura Cunningham stated that if the present trend continues, "By 1990 everyone in the United States will be living alone." She says:

In Manhattan the average household is already whittled down to 1.96. What does 1.96 mean? No matter how you slice it, 1.96 is not a couple. "No," you say to yourself, "1.96 is just an average. There are still couples." You've probably even seen them in the elevator of your building and in lines in front of Cinema I, and it's true. There are a few couples left, but they won't stay together much longer. It's doubtful that Manhattan can hold the line at 1.96 through the winter: We could attain the 1.0 household by Lincoln's birthday. A few insensitive remarks, a Perrier bottle hurled at the wall, and there you have it: 1.0.

According to the census (1980) more Americans have been leaving one another in the last ten years than ever before in our nation's history. Swallow hard and look at the facts. In 1917 the average household was 3.11, in 1980, 2.75. Yet in this period, the number of households shot up by 27 percent. You don't have to be a mathematical genius to see what's coming up. At this rate, it's going to be just you, Babe . . . as the divorce rate has soared, the birthrate has dropped, so, what we can expect to see is fewer children of more broken homes. These children of divorce will be in transit until they can afford to avoid both parents' homes, in favor of solitary quarters of their own. The "single parent" home can then become the "empty nest." The puzzle is that empty though the nest may be, the number of nests keeps rising: from 63.4 million to 80.4 million in the last decade.[5]

The grim humor of that quote pinpoints a salient fact: Marriage, which God intended to be a lifelong relationship, has been devastated by modern man with the result that man, who was given a woman to fulfill and complete him, is now "going it alone," walking away from his God-given responsibility.

Nor has the Christian home resisted this trend. A frightening number of Christian men and women are choosing to float downstream with a deteriorating society rather than fight upstream to spawn a new generation of stability.

A recent article in *Christianity Today* suggests that clergy divorce has at least quadrupled since 1960.[6] It points out that in one organization, 37 percent of the clergy are seriously considering divorce, while over 60 percent have marriage problems "serious enough to make divorce a distinct possibility." One Christian conference center has had a long-standing policy forbidding the use of divorced speakers on its program. Recently there has been pressure to change this historic position. The reason? Because many of the popular conference speakers on the circuit today are now divorced. It is said that "among professionals, clergymen rank third in the number of divorces granted each year."[7]

Mary LaGrand Bouma in her book, *Divorce in the Parsonage*,[8] strips off the veneer and lays bare the core of the problem. In interviewing nearly 200 pastors, wives, ex-pastors, and ex-wives, she unfolds the horror story of professing Christians who have rationalized that the commitment to "love, honor, and cherish till death do us part" did not need to be kept by them because their situation was "exceptional." The fact is that even pastors are beginning to buy the Hollywood standard of marriage and the Playboy philosophy of selfish personal fulfillment.

One denomination established a hotline to provide ministers and their wives with the names of marriage counselors in their area. In this particular denomination fifty ministers in the northern part of one state were divorced in the last decade. Reference was made to this fact by a woman writing to Ann Landers.

She concluded her letter by asking, "For God's sake, Ann, if the clergy can't keep their marriages together, who can?"[9]

Foundation of Society

When one considers the signs of our times, it calls to mind the desperate question David posed in Psalm 11:3, "If the foundations are destroyed, what can the righteous do?" The very foundation of society is marriage, the home, and the family. If this foundation is destroyed we are set adrift on the sea of human solutions that never work. The psalmist answers his question:

> The Lord is in His holy temple . . . on His heavenly throne. He observes the sons of men; His eyes examine them. The Lord examines the righteous, but the wicked and those who love violence His soul hates. . . . For the Lord is righteous, He loves justice; upright men will see His face (Psalm 11:4-5, 7, NIV).

It is the privilege of those committed to divine truth to look away from the crumbling, deteriorating, eroding standards of our day, and see the face of our Lord who is the "same yesterday and today, yes and forever" (Hebrews 13:8). We look to God who says, "I, the Lord, do not change" (Malachi 3:6) to the One "with whom there is no variation, or shifting shadow" (James 1:17), and what do we discover? "The righteous Lord loveth righteousness" (Psalm 11:7, KJV). For a culture that has lost its way, there is direction. In a society with no foundation, "The firm foundation of God stands" (2 Timothy 2:19). The foundation of marriage is the righteous standard of the righteous Lord.

Psalm 127:1 reveals, "Unless the Lord builds the house, they labor in vain who build it." The psalmist goes on to show that it is pointless to rise up early or stay up late or even work extra hard trying to accomplish something without the blessing of God.

God's idea of marriage is a permanent relationship with one person for life. Divorce is not an option in the divine ideal. Consider the evidence: When God originated marriage He set the pattern. In Genesis 2:24 God declared that the spouses were to cleave. Cleaving is an essential element in the covenant language of the Old Testament. It denotes a permanent bond of unity and oneness. By stating that a man is to "cleave" to his wife, God is emphasizing that he is to hang on to her at all cost in a wholehearted commitment.

Divorce Trauma

Alex and Barbara had just obtained a divorce when Barbara came for counsel. Her description of the intense suffering she was facing was graphic: "I feel as though I am torn apart and only half of me has survived." Psychologists are more and more recognizing that a divorce does the kind of damage emotionally that even the loss of a partner in death does not do. Some liken the recovery from a divorce trauma to a drug addict being helped down from a "high." Edward Beal, M.D., Clinical Assistant Professor at Georgetown University Family Center in Washington, D.C., has studied lifelong morbidity and mortality patterns of people who are single, married, divorced, and remarried. He concluded that especially for males, divorce "is highly correlated with both an increased morbidity and early death."[10] Erica Abeel, a divorced college professor, said, "Divorce is a disaster, a malady, and women suffer from a tremendous overload, one that could easily make you 'crazy.' "[11]

Counselors are trying an endless list of gimmicks to "reduce the trauma of divorce."

• Divorce ceremonies to ask God's "blessing" on the dissolution of a marriage

• Creating "widowhood fantasies" so that emotionally the person thinks of the former mate as "dead" and thus accepts the divorce better

• Dealing with guilt by reprogramming the mind to accept divorce as inevitable.

These are only a few of the many attempts to "help" divorced people. One wonders if it has ever occurred to the
counselors that the best help of all is God's plan of keeping the
marriage together, working out the problems, forgiving, giving
a little, and ordering your life around God's priorities. Is it too
simplistic to say that the need for divorce therapy would be
greatly reduced if divorce were reduced?

One-Flesh Concept

God said, "They shall become one flesh" (Genesis 2:24). One
cannot be divided and maintain wholeness. When God made
Adam, He saw that wholeness could only be achieved by the
addition of another person. Completeness is found in the marriage relationship a man has with his wife.

Allen Ross says, "To become one flesh means becoming a
spiritual, moral, intellectual, and physical unity."[12] Ross also
points out that "this unity is seen in the sharing of the same
name, the same home and worldly goods, being parents of the
same children, being partners in joy and sorrow."[13] Abel Isaksson points out that the term "one flesh" actually refers to a
kinship that is so permanent that even if the husband or wife
dies, the other is not free to marry those of the partner's family
without committing incest. That seems to be the best explanation for the prohibition of relationships of affinity in Leviticus
18. In any event, there is no doubt that becoming "one flesh"
involves a definite change from singleness to unity.[14]

When you find Genesis 2:24 quoted in the New Testament
no fewer than three times, the continuing biblical doctrine of
permanence in marriage becomes even more evident.

Paul quotes it in Ephesians 5:31 to show that marriage illustrates the body of Christ. He points out that a man should love
and care for his wife as he does for his own physical body,
because after marriage she is in essence his own body, just as
the church is the body of Christ. Then he quotes Genesis
2:24. Marriage by its very nature of oneness and unity and

permanence provides us with an illustration of the oneness, unity, and permanence that exists in the body of Christ.

That truth comes into clear focus in Mark 10:8-9. After rebuking the Pharisees for their hardhearted interpretation of the Mosaic law, Jesus quoted Genesis 2:24 and added two conclusions:

• "Consequently they are no longer two, but one flesh." By repeating with emphasis this phrase, Christ was declaring that a real difference takes place in the marriage relationship. He did not say, "The *goal* of marriage is oneness," but rather confirmed that the *result* of marriage is oneness. Oneness is established by God and must be guarded (Ephesians 4:3).

• "What therefore God has joined together, let no man separate." Christ makes clear that God is sovereign in the marriage and man is not. Man quite simply does not have the right to dismantle the "one flesh" that God has established. People who seek divorce as a solution to their problems, the pastors, attorneys, and counselors who encourage people to divorce, and the judges who grant divorces are clearly acting contrary to God's Word.

The Permanence of Marriage

In Matthew's account of the same confrontation, the kibitzing Pharisees tried to challenge the clear word of Christ by putting Moses on the spot. In essence they were saying, "But Moses allowed it" (Matthew 19:7). Christ's rejoinder should slow down the most avid divorce advocate. "Because of your hardness of heart, Moses permitted you to divorce your wives; but from the beginning it has not been this way" (Matthew 19:8).

The so-called "Mosaic permission" (which we will discuss more fully in a later chapter) was not quite as simple as the Pharisees made it. To recognize divorce as an option is tantamount to admitting hardness of heart because of an unwillingness to hear God's Word or heed God's will.

But Christ presents a clear alternative—the message for

those whose hearts are tender and who have a listening ear: "From the beginning it has not been this way." Christ tells those who want to listen of the divine ideal established at the beginning of human history. When the righteous standard of God, His plumbline, is held against the standard of man, man's desires are found to be out of line.

Another very important text on the permanent nature of marriage is found in Malachi. The prophet was pointing out the reasons God had withheld His blessing from His people. Skillfully using a question-and-answer method, God indicted Israel for cheating (1:6-14), unfaithfulness (2:1-9), mixed marriage (2:10-12), divorce (2:13-16), impiety (2:17), robbing God (3:7-12), and arrogance (3:13-15).

The section in Malachi 2:13-16 is one of the most profound texts in Scripture on the subject of marriage permanence. The people came to the altar of the Lord with tears and groaning and weeping so that the fire on the altar was extinguished by their tears. But God did not respond and the people asked, "Why?" (vv. 13-14)

Malachi put his finger on a very tender nerve: "Because the Lord has been a witness between you and the wife of your youth, against whom you have dealt treacherously" (v. 14). God's witness against these people and the reason for withholding His blessing was their failure to face up to the seriousness of divorce. Perhaps some were saying as people do today, "We were very young when we got married and we really did not understand what we were doing."

God called it "treachery" ("breaking faith," NIV) no less than three times (2:14-16). Twice He referred to the woman who was divorced as "the wife of thy youth." In the mind of God a divorce did not close the matter. He reminded the people through His prophet, "She is your companion."

The Hebrew word for *companion* used here is not the usual word for an associate or partner but rather an intense word meaning "knit together." The NIV translates the word "partner," but even that is not strong enough. The feminine form is found only here in the Old Testament, but the masculine form and the root are used often. One lexicon suggests the meaning of the root is "to unite, tie a magic knot."[15] It speaks of being closely woven together. It includes both the thought of joining together in a common enterprise and joining in a contract and mutual commitment to each other. The word is related to a common Semitic root meaning "to be joined," and translates as "bind" in Assyrian. It is used to speak of objects joined together (Exodus 26:3; 28:7), military alliances (Genesis 14:3; 2 Chronicles 20:35-37), men joined together in the human race (Ecclesiastes 9:4) or in a community (Psalm 122:3), and in commitment to a religious system (Hosea 4:17; Psalm 94:20). It describes the bond Daniel had with his three friends because of common faith and loyalty to God (Daniel 2:13-18). Psalm 119:63 states that fear of God is the common bond between "companions."[16]

Then Malachi adds, "She is . . . your wife by covenant." Divorce quite simply is not consistent with the covenantal nature of marriage. The wedding vows are inviolable from God's perspective. The warning in Proverbs 2:16-19 against the harlot points out that in resorting to harlotry, she "leaves the companion of her youth [her husband] and forgets the covenant of her God [her wedding vows]."

Malachi then reinforces the covenantal nature of marriage in four ways.

1. Breaking faith with one's marriage partner is not consistent with the presence of God's Holy Spirit in one's life. Malachi 2:15 says, "But not one has done so who has a remnant of the Spirit." Or, "No one with a remnant of the Spirit of God or respect for God's law would do this."

2. God provided oneness in marriage because His purpose is the raising up of a godly seed.[17] "And what did that one do while he was seeking a godly offspring?"

3. God despises divorce. " 'For I hate divorce,' says the Lord, the God of Israel" (v. 16).

4. Breaking faith with your marriage partner is said to remove the partner's protection, thus treating such a one cruelly. "For I hate . . . him who covers his garment with wrong" (v. 16). This likely refers to the ancient custom of putting a garment over a woman to claim her as wife (see Deuteronomy 22:30; Ruth 3:9; Psalm 73:6; Ezekiel 16:8). But instead of spreading a garment to protect their wives, the men of Malachi's day covered their garments with violence toward their wives, ignoring the hurt and tears and emotional damage that divorce brings.

Foundation for Marriage

The goal of every believer should be a growing maturity in his Christian life. This means, among other things, to "walk" (keep step) "in the Spirit" of God (Galatians 5:16), superimpose God's will and desire over his own (Luke 22:42 with Romans 12:1-2), hate what God hates (Psalm 119:104, 128), and refuse to do harm to others (1 John 3:7-11). Since divorce is inconsistent with these principles, it is inconceivable that we as believers should ever recommend or participate in divorce. The undergirding of our society is the home and the family, and the foundation of the family must be God's infallible Word.

The Sermon on the Mount presents a path of righteousness for disciples. Its demands include a righteousness that exceeds the righteousness of the scribes and the Pharisees (Matthew 5:20). It clearly presents a standard that far surpasses the legalistic yet convenient traditions of man. What Christ presented to His disciples is revolutionary today, just as it was in His time. At the end of this discourse Christ said:

> "Therefore every one who hears these words of Mine, and acts upon them, may be compared to a wise man, who built his house upon the rock. And the rain descended, and the floods came, and the winds blew, and burst against that house; and yet it did not fall, for it had been founded upon the rock.

And every one who hears these words of Mine, and does not act upon them, will be like a foolish man, who built his house upon the sand. And the rain descended, and the floods came, and the winds blew, and burst against that house; and it fell, and great was its fall" (Matthew 7:24-27).

His words are difficult and cut across popular notions of men. They contradict even what religious leaders teach; but the bottom line is this: If you hear and act on His Word, you have a foundation on which to build. If you hear but do not act on it, you will build on the shifting sands of human reasoning and your house will fall.

God's Word declares that marriage is permanent. The marriage covenant is permanent, with no exceptions in the fine print. God does not provide us with an escape hatch or a loophole in the laws of matrimony. If you obey God's Word, no matter what the outward circumstances, you will build on a sure foundation, and no storm of life can shake you. But if you purpose to ignore the truth of God's Word, everything you build will be vulnerable to the winds and the floods, and your house will fall and great will be its fall.

God Hates Divorce

John and Joan were new Christians facing the struggles that often accompany believers' baby steps. Their marriage was in trouble. It had been shaky before salvation and accepting Christ at a city-wide evangelistic meeting did not prove to be the cure-all they expected. Several books came into their hands which seemed to say that, while divorce for a Christian was not recommended, there were exceptions. In some cases, they read, it is best for all concerned to call it quits and get a fresh start. They were convinced that theirs was such a case.

One Sunday they heard me say in a morning message that "God hates divorce." The statement was only mentioned once as an illustration that God often hates what we so easily accept, but it hit both of them between the eyes and the next week we met to discuss it.

When I shared the consistent teaching of the Bible on the subject of the permanence of marriage, John squared his broad shoulders and managed to force a grin. He looked at Joan and said, "I guess we're stuck with each other for the rest of our lives, Babe. Let's call a truce and see if we can't learn to love each other again." I laughed and said, "Well, that's a start." With a fresh resolve, and believing that only death should end their marriage, they were forced to try. With counsel, the reading of Dr. Ed Wheat's book, *Love Life for Every Married Couple,* and God's help, they discovered a relationship they never dreamed possible. John said to me not long ago, "Pastor, if you had left one loophole in your stand on marriage, we would have taken it and missed the greatest joy in our life. When we were 'trapped' with no way out, we both got on the right side of our problems and discovered they were not as big as we thought."

> Got any rivers you think are uncrossable?
> Got any mountains you can't tunnel thru?
> God specializes in things thought impossible.
> He does the things others cannot do.[18]

FOOTNOTES

1. Rafe Vanhoy, *What's Forever For?* Tree Publishing Co., Inc., Nashville, 1978.
2. Neile Adams, quoted in Marilyn Beck's Hollywood (Syndicated column), *San Jose Mercury News,* September 18, 1971, p. 27.

3. L.B. Franche, et al., "The Children of Divorce," *Newsweek,* February 11, 1980.
4. Ellen A. Adamoyurka, "Treating the Stresses of Remarried Families," *Marriage and Divorce Today,* (newsletter), Atcom, Inc., New York, March 22, 1982, p. 1.
5. Laura Cunningham, "Lifestyle—A Couple Years More and We'll be Living as One," *Chicago Tribune,* November 8, 1981.
6. Robert J. Stout, "Clergy Divorce Spills Into the Aisle," *Christianity Today,* February 5, 1982.
7. Lucille Lavender, *They Cry Too,* Hawthorne Books, Inc., p. 97.
8. Mary LaGrand Bouma, *Divorce in the Parsonage,* (Minneapolis: Bethany Fellowship, 1979).
9. Ann Landers (Syndicated column), *San Jose Mercury News,* March 11, 1979.
10. Edward Beal, quoted in "Divorce, Especially Harmful to Health of Males," *Marriage and Divorce Today,* (newsletter), Atcom, Inc., New York, May 31, 1982.
11. Erica Abeel, quoted in "The Divorced Woman—Trying to Juggle Her Many Roles," *Current Research on Marriage, Families, and Divorce,* (Manual), Atcom Publishing Co., New York, 1979, p. 40.
12. Allen P. Ross, "Woman: In the Beginning," *Kindred Spirit,* Dallas Theological Seminary, Winter 1980, p. 10.
13. Ibid.
14. Abel Isaksson, *Marriage and Ministry in the New Temple,* Neil Tomkinson (trans.) with assistance of Jean Gray, (Lund: Gleerup; Copenhagen: Munksgaard, 1965), pp. 20-24.
15. Francis Brown, S.R. Driver, and Charles A. Briggs, *Hebrew and English Lexicon of the Old Testament,* (London: Oxford University, Clarendon Press, 1972).
16. R.L. Harris, G.L. Archer, Jr., and B.K. Waltke (eds.), *Theological Wordbook of the Old Testament,* Vol. 1, (Chicago: Moody Press, 1980), p. 260.

17. Some see this as a reference to the fact that God only made one woman and one man, even though He had enough power (residue of the Spirit) to create more wives if He wished. Why did He only create one? Polygamy and divorce are not conducive to nurturing children in the fear of God and God desired a godly seed. See: Charles L. Feinberg, *The Minor Prophets,* (Chicago: Moody Press, 1980), p. 258.
18. Oscar Eliason, *Got Any Rivers?* Singspiration, Inc., (Grand Rapids: Zondervan Publishing House, 1945). Used by permission.

7

Satan's Strategy

Psychology Today recently ran an article in which Chris Cox suggested a Golden Rule test. Basing his article on the work of psychologist Bernard Rimland of the Institute for Child Behavior Research in San Diego, Cox stated that the happiest people are those who help others.

Dr. Rimland's suggestion was that you make a list of the ten people you know best. After each name, write either H (happy) or N (unhappy). Then go through the list again, this time writing either S (selfish) or U (unselfish) by the names. Dr. Rimland defines selfishness as "a stable tendency to devote one's time and resources to one's own interests and welfare—an unwillingness to inconvenience oneself for others."

Dr. Rimland had examined the cases of 1,988 people rated by 216 students in his college classes. He found that in only 78 of these cases were people rated as both happy and selfish. The rest fell into either the happy or the unselfish pattern. The paradox that Cox suggests is that selfish people are by definition devoted to bringing themselves happiness. Judged by others, however, they seem to succeed less often than people who work at bringing happiness to others. His conclusion, "Do unto others as you would have them do unto you."[1]

"Be Selfish"

As I waited in line at the grocery store, the headline in the newsrack caught my eye. "Kate Jackson's Formula for a Happy Marriage: Be Selfish." The article, written by Fred Robbins, quoted film and television star Kate Jackson as saying that the only way she can be a wife and actress and be happy is to be selfish. "Everything's got to be for you first," said the wife of Andrew Stevens. She went on to explain:

> If you don't make Number One happy—and you know who Number One is—you'll never make anyone else happy. You've got to be selfish, to a certain extent. You've got to make yourself happy first. It's up to you—and you alone. But I truly do not believe that you can make another person happy. You simply must make yourself happy—and hope.[2]

Apparently Kate Jackson's formula did not work—she recently announced that she and Stevens were getting a divorce.

Dr. Hans Selye, a physician in Montreal seems to agree with this philosophy. In his book, *Stress Without Distress,* he prescribes "a strong dose of selfishness" as the best way of achieving a happier, saner society. Dr. Selye suggests that "unbridled idealism is a cancerous curse" and he says that the biblical injunction, "Thou shalt love thy neighbor as thyself," is a biological heresy." The doctor asserts that true self-interest covers the full range of biological drives, including man's social nature and his need to get along with other people. The solution he offers is "altruistic egotism" which he defines as "helping others for the selfish motive of deserving help in return."[3]

The "be selfish" philosophy of life did not originate with Kate Jackson or Dr. Hans Selye. The author and promoter of that lie was Satan himself. The Bible records his selfish plans. Five times he said, "I will," revealing his agenda for self-exaltation:

> I will ascend to heaven;
> I will raise my throne above the stars of God,

And I will sit on the mount of assembly
In the recesses of the north.
I will ascend above the heights of the clouds;
I will make myself like the Most High (Isaiah 14:13-14).

The success of this program which Satan insinuated into the human race in the Garden of Eden is evident from the annals of history. Self-centeredness planted in the heart of man was behind the Fall of man (Genesis 3), the murder of Abel (Genesis 4), the sin of Noah's generation (Genesis 6), the building of Babel (Genesis 11), and myraid other incidents involving every tragic event in the course of human history.

What is the source of quarrels and conflicts among you? Is not the source your pleasures [NIV, "desires"; KJV, "lusts"] that wage war in your members? You lust and do not have; so you commit murder. And you are envious and cannot obtain; so you fight and quarrel" (James 4:1-2).

Looking over the titles in one section of a bookstore, I saw the following:
The Art of Selfishness
Winning Thru Intimidation
The New Assertive Woman
Looking Out for #1
Stand Up—Speak Out—Talk Back!
The dust cover on that last title added, "Are you in charge of your own life? Or do other people run it? Learn how to stand up for yourself—get what you want—without anger, fear, or guilt."[4] (See Romans 15:2-3.)

The Lie of Independence
With books like these promoting selfish attitudes and actions, it is no wonder we are in trouble today. Satan offers selfishness as a panacea for all the world's ills. He decided to live independently of God (Isaiah 14:13-14). He persuaded Eve that she

could "do her thing" and be independent of God. This is what the Bible calls "the lie." Jesus said of Satan:

> He was a murderer from the beginning, and does not stand in the truth, because there is no truth in him. Whenever he speaks a lie, he speaks from his own nature; for he is a liar, and the father of lies (John 8:44).

Paul wrote that the unbeliever exchanges the truth of God for a lie (Romans 1:25). He also predicted that because people do not "receive the love of the truth . . . God will send upon them a deluding influence so that they might believe what is false" (lit., "the lie," 2 Thessalonians 2:10-11).

The essence of that satanic lie is that man can be selfishly independent. When man begins to believe that he can be autonomous from God, he seeks to be autonomous in human relationships as well. Late in the nineteenth century, Friedrich Wilhelm Nietzsche wrote about the "rugged individualist" and the "self-made man." He believed that God was dead and that Christianity was a "slave morality." In other words, it prevented a person from "doing his thing." Our modern society has been saturated with this "me first" idea and we are reaping its grim result.

A recent manual for an industrial motivational seminar quotes a poem by Diane Tice which sums up the "me first" idea:[5]

> I have been my own prisoner.
> Who am I to have so pompously bestowed
>   Upon my self a life sentence of
>   _____ ?
>   (you fill in the blank)
> I have been a judge and jury and given
>   myself that sentence to a prison of
>   my own making.
> But, because I am my own judge and jury,
>   I can commute my own sentence and
>   set myself free!

Self-Centeredness

Selfish independence, which J. Allan Petersen calls "the biggest problem in marriage,"[6] tears at the very heart of the home. It erodes the purpose of God which requires us to be dependent creatures, and it destroys the healthy interdependence God established in human relationships. It militates against real love, because love "does not seek its own" (1 Corinthians 13:5).

Walt Kelley perceptively has Pogo say, "We have met the enemy and he is us!" "A man is his own worst enemy" is more than an adage. It contains much truth. When a person takes but does not give, he becomes stagnant like the Dead Sea. W.E. Gladstone, British statesman of the last century said, "The greatest curse of the human race is selfishness."

Even secular marriage counselors are beginning to see the futility of the "me-first" posture as a "way of trying to manage our own lives."[7] One such writer offers case histories of frustrated people who centered their lives around themselves and then warns,

> Our society is littered with the debris of marital or quasimarital relationships caught in the whirlwind of me-first survival strategies like the typical instances I have listed above. The people who take this road to marital happiness eventually arrive at a dead end. For acting on the assumption that one's spouse exists solely to make one happy results in making two persons miserable.[8]

Psychologist David G. Meyers recently pointed out that while there has been great emphasis on building self-esteem, research psychologists have been gathering new data to prove that "the most common error is 'self-serving bias'—not an inferiority complex, but a superiority complex."[9]

The Bible makes clear that the blight of self-centeredness afflicts the inner man. An evidence of our sinful condition is that "each of us has turned to his own way" (Isaiah 53:6). Paul said of people in his day that they did not genuinely care for the welfare of others: "For they all seek after their own interests" (Philippians 2:21). Like the mythological Narcissus we look into the pool, fall in love with our own reflection, and pine away in our egotistical infatuation.

One of Aesop's Fables tells of a dog who stole a piece of meat which he firmly held in his mouth as he ran away with it. He came to a stream which was bridged over by a log. Seeing what he thought was another dog holding a piece of meat in his mouth, he greedily opened his mouth to grab the other dog's meat. Of course, what he saw was merely his own reflection; through his greed, he lost what he had.

Barbara sat in my office with tears streaming down her face. Frank had walked out an hour before and Barbara's sand castle had been washed out to sea. "How could I have been so stupid?" she moaned. "I wanted to have my cake and eat it too. Frank was so nice. I kept just pushing, pushing, pushing, and finally I pushed too far."

In the marriage relationship two people must come together with a desire to say no to selfish desires and wants and a determination to live with a constant care and concern for one's mate. Selfish attitudes will soon erode the beauty of marital love. You cannot just push to get your own way and expect to find happiness.

Dora was married for the third time. Now that marriage was close to divorce. What was the problem? In her words, "I just must have my own way, but when I get it I no longer have someone with whom I can share it."

Bill wept as he confessed, "Jean left me last night. The last thing she said was, 'You are the most selfish man I ever met.' I guess she is right; we both wanted our way. Now that does not seem too important."

Then there is Helen who, after four marriages, admits that if she had to do it over, she would stay with her first husband. "Each marriage has been a greater disaster. I thought I knew what I wanted, but it has just gone from bad to worse."

In examining hundreds of cases of marital conflict, I have found selfishness to be a villain in all of them. "Where there is selfishness there is bound to be disagreement, conflict, and separation. Wars start right here, whether on a world scale or in one individual marriage."[10]

Selfishness motivates one to take another man's car, another man's life, or another man's wife, and selfishness fills the courts of our land with thieves, murderers, and adulterers.

It was selfishness that motivated Jeff to come home in the middle of the night, wake up his wife of 18 months, and announce: "I don't want to be married any more—it cramps my style."

If the divorce courts had a rule that only unselfish people could get divorces, it would sound the death knell for divorce.

Why do people divorce?

"I want my rights!"

"He has no business treating me that way!"

"I have to think of my happiness!"

"If she is going to do her thing—I'm going to do mine!"

"I can't take it any more."

I. Me. My. Mine.

> There is a foe whose hidden power
>   The Christian may well fear.
> More subtle far than inbred sin,
>   And to the heart more dear.
> It is the power of selfishness,
>   It is the willful "I"
> And ere my Lord can live in me,
>   My very self must die.
> —Author unknown

The simple fact remains that selfishness is the very essence of sin. God despises the attitudes of self-centeredness that are so prevalent today, and He grieves as the fruit of that selfish lifestyle eats away at the very foundation of all relationships.

Christ Our Example

The Apostle Paul wrote, "Now the deeds of the flesh are evident," and then he listed fifteen selfish qualities (Galatians 5:19):

- Self-centered sexual life—immorality, impurity, sensuality
- Self-centered spiritual life—idolatry, sorcery
- Self-centered social life—enmities, strife, jealousy, outbursts of anger, disputes, dissensions, factions, envying, drunkenness, carousing.

He contrasted this with the unselfish lifestyle produced by the Spirit—love, joy, peace, patience, kindness, goodness, faithfulness, gentleness, self-control. Then he said, "Now those who belong to Christ Jesus have crucified the flesh with its passions and desires.... Let us not become boastful, challenging one another, envying one another" (Galatians 5:19-26).

Christ, the perfect God-man, was selfless. He lived for others (Acts 10:38), took on Himself the suffering and sorrows and even the sin of all of us (Isaiah 53:5-6), and bestowed on us all of heaven's bounty. He who was rich became poor so we could be rich (2 Corinthians 8:9). His pattern of thought, word, and deed was God first, others second. His own comforts and desires were put aside.

But the servant is not greater than His Lord (John 13:16). Jesus said, "If anyone wishes to come after Me, let him deny himself" (Matthew 16:24). Paul gives a major key to all human relationships: "We then ought ... not just please ourselves" (Romans 15:1).

When a husband is constantly reflecting the unselfish attitudes of Christ—constantly saying no to his own desires and constantly pleasing his wife—he will cheat the divorce courts. When a wife does the same, divorce attorneys will have to look for a new line of work. When we consider the shipwreck we see in modern marriage we have to be concerned. Since selfishness is at the root of the divorce problem, we must not take a position on this subject that will aid and abet those who want to go their own selfish way. It is often much easier to just follow the current trends and float downstream with the crowd.

Recently we saw a copy of an ad that was said to have run in *TV Guide*. While we couldn't get in touch with John-Michael Productions who placed the ad, the following seems to speak for itself. The ad pictures a ring with a broken band and reads,

YOU SURVIVED ... It wasn't easy. But you made it through an experience which probably held the most magical *and* the most painful moments of your entire life. A marriage. And now it's over.

And though you may have sometimes doubted it, the experience did *not* destroy you. In fact, you're stronger now than ever before.

You are a survivor. And you'll never be the same again.

If you're ready to let the world know it, and if you you feel like making a very special, a very *personal* declaration of independence, now you can ... with the new DIVORCE RING® band.

Wear it as a symbol of your strength, your independence, and your availability. The DIVORCE RING® band is a terrific conversation starter. And more, it's a strong signal to others like yourself that you're entering the future optimistically and unafraid.

The stunning DIVORCE RING® band is made of 14k gold electroplate and is available in sizes 5-12. And the good news is that it can be yours for only $39.95. For those wanting an added investment, it's also available in 10k and 14k solid gold.

Order your DIVORCE RING® band today ... *Now* is the time to celebrate your new beginning.[11]

When a person is divorced, the reasons given for a desire to remarry are often just as selfish as the ones given for divorce.

Connie is just 24 but already divorced and, by her own admission, "husband hunting." Her words express the hidden motive behind many remarriage attempts: "I have had one unhappy marriage and I deserve better. I have needs, you know, and my happiness is too important for me to be sentenced to the single life." Does that sound as if she is indeed prepared to deny herself and "take up her cross and follow" Christ? Whatever the solution to the divorce/remarriage problem, it must be in line with an unselfish resolve to do God's will, no matter what the cost.

"Far too many people, Christians not excluded," says Geoffrey Bromiley, "are self-centeredly preoccupied with their own marital problems and their attempt to engineer solutions to them."[12] Rather than "engineering" selfish solutions we must find biblical solutions. But that is always hard on human ego. The way of the Christian is the way of self-denial (Matthew 16:24; Luke 14:26-27). It is the way of the Saviour who "did not please Himself" (Romans 15:3).

A Parable of Love

William Sidney Porter, master of the short story and better known under the pseudonym O. Henry, tells a delightful tale of Della and Jim who married in virtual poverty. The only assets they could call their own were Della's long, beautiful hair and Jim's beautiful gold watch given to him by his father. Christmas presented a dilemma—each desired to bestow a token of love on the other.

Della, with only a meager $1.85, decided to sell her hair for $20 and buy a fob for Jim's treasured watch. When Jim came home and saw Della without her beautiful hair, he gasped but loved her all the more. Then he handed Della her gift—a set of expensive tortoiseshell combs, set with jewels for her lovely hair. He had sold his prized watch to buy them for her.

The unselfish lovers had given to each other all they had to give—their very best. This attitude obliterates the very premise on which divorce is based.

FOOTNOTES

1. Chris Cox, "A Golden Rule Test," *Psychology Today,* December 1982, p. 78.
2. Fred Robbins, *The National Enquirer,* December 1979, p. 19.
3. Hans Selye, *Stress Without Distress,* (New York: The New American Library, Inc., 1975).
4. Robert Alberti and Michael Emmons, *Stand Up—Speak Out—Talk Back!* (New York: Pocket Books, 1975).
5. Louis Tice, *New Age Thinking for Achieving Your Potential,* (manual), (Seattle: The Pacific Institute, Inc., 1980), p. 21-23. Used by permission.
6. J. Allan Petersen, "The Biggest Problem in Marriage," *Family and Marriage Success* (workbook), Family Concern, Inc., (Omaha, Nebraska, 1972), p. 5.
7. Mel Krantzler, *Creative Marriage,* (New York: McGraw-Hill, 1981), p. 14.
8. Ibid., p. 17.
9. David G. Meyers, *Evangelical Newsletter,* Evangelical Ministries, Inc., Philadelphia, July 1982.
10. J. Allan Petersen, "The Biggest Problem in Marriage," p. 16.
11. *The Wittenburg Door,* No. 65, February/March 1982, p. 24, quoting an ad from *TV Guide.*
12. Geoffrey Bromiley, *God and Marriage,* (Grand Rapids: Wm. B. Eerdmans Publishing Co., 1980), p. xii.

8

A Survey of
Divorce Views

Divorce is a major social problem today. America has more than 1.6 million divorced citizens. The nation is more conscious of divorce than ever before.

> Books on how to initiate and survive divorce are crowding sex manuals in the book stores. Divorce insurance is being promoted by some feminists, lawyers, and legislators. Divorce greeting cards toast the uncoupling.[1]

Dr. Donald B. Louria is not completely pessimistic about the future of the family, but he is discouraged and believes that time is running out. Dr. Louria, head of the New Jersey Medical School's Department of Preventive Medicine and Community Health, says, "Now we have about one-third of families breaking up—a difficult problem, but one that can be dealt with." But he is more pessimistic about the future, believing that if the divorce rate increases to the 55 percent range, the broken family will be so much a part of the American scene that no steps will suffice to preserve the family's existence.[2]

Psychologist Albert Ellis wrote, "People are not truly monogamous and romantic love is not durable. . . . Romantic love tends to last no more than three to five years, especially if the participants are under the same roof."[3]

Because the world has no absolutes, it is subject to the whims and the capricious nature of man. It is no wonder that an increasingly amoral society has received homosexuality, abortion, premarital sex, and divorce as "acceptable lifestyles." These things should be expected, for the Bible predicts them.

In 2 Timothy 3, Paul spoke of difficult days ahead which would be marked by the following characteristics:

> For men will be lovers of self, lovers of money, boastful, arrogant, revilers, disobedient to parents, ungrateful, unholy, unloving, irreconcilable, malicious gossips, without self-control, brutal, haters of good, treacherous, reckless, conceited, lovers of pleasure rather than lovers of God (2 Timothy 3:2-4).

In going through that list, one cannot help but be impressed with how many of them relate to the issue of divorce. Consider, for example, the self-centeredness we talked about in the last chapter. Marriages are often brought to ruin through men being "lovers of self . . . boastful, arrogant . . . conceited." Material things often bring strain on relationships. An article in *Reader's Digest* in 1969 reported that half of the couples who come to Family Service agencies for counseling report severe problems with money.[4] The problem: "For men will be . . . lovers of money."

How much does lack of love come into play in marital tension? "Men will be . . . unloving."

Have you ever heard of divorce for irreconcilable differences? "Men shall be irreconcilable."[5] When we consider this text, it is easy to see why divorce is emerging as a major problem in this generation.

A Relaxed Church

But while the social trend is not surprising, the great concern today is the compromising tendency of the evangelical church.

Elton Trueblood in *The Incendiary Fellowship* points out that the church is in trouble when it stops being in tension with the current attitudes of the culture.[6] We are certainly seeing that relaxed tension becoming a reality. Christ warned, "If the salt has become tasteless ... it is good for nothing" (Matthew 5:13). Dr. James Dobson claims that the divorce rate for Christians is nearly as high as for the population at large.[7]

Dwight Hervey Small calls divorce and remarriage "a disruption, technically sinful in view of God's pure, creative intent."[8] This kind of "theological double talk"[9] has led evangelical writers, pastors, and counselors to take an increasingly free stand on this subject—from allowing divorce and remarriage in certain "special circumstances" (such as Chuck Swindoll in *Strike the Original Match* or John MacArthur in *The Family*) to a wide open policy of "grace covers all" (such as *Remarriage, A Healing Gift From God* by Larry Richards).

Because this is such an emotional subject, there is the danger that the debate will produce more heat than light. Those who allow divorce and remarriage are criticized for being too loose, and those who do not allow them are accused of being legalistic and uncaring. Fortunately, we do have an authority on the subject that gives us some absolutes. No amount of theological juggling or exegetical gymnastics can remove the clear fact that the preponderance of biblical data teaches clearly that God's best is one man for one woman until death. This was God's original design and, though it has been violated regularly through the ages, the design has never changed.

When God dealt directly with those who compromised this standard in Malachi's day, He pointed out that the sin of divorce retards one's spiritual life and communion with God (as does other sin), that it is treachery toward one's mate and the breaking of a covenant. And then He stated unequivocally, "I hate divorce" (Malachi 2:14-16).

When Christ confronted the Pharisees directly on this subject (Matthew 19 and Mark 10), He forced them to view the divine ideal in Genesis 2 and then added, "What therefore God has joined together, let no man separate." When they hedged by appealing to the so-called Mosaic permission, He stated, "From the beginning it has not been this way" (Matthew 19:6, 8). In Ephesians 5 the Apostle Paul offers the insight that marriage is an earthly illustration of the divine relationship Christ has with His church. Among the several explicit comparisons that are made, the implication of a permanent conjoining is clear.

Paul's reiteration of the Lord's teaching concludes, "The wife should not leave her husband (but if she does leave, let her remain unmarried, or else be reconciled to her husband), and that the husband should not send his wife away" (1 Corinthians 7:10-11). This is, without question, the ideal that God has declared in His Word. What then gives rise to the less strict view of divorce and remarriage? The debate has centered around three basic issues:

• The meaning of the divorce permission in the Mosaic law (Deuteronomy 24:1-4).

• The meaning of Matthew's exception clauses, "except for immorality" (Matthew 19:9); "except for the cause of unchastity" (Matthew 5:32).

• The meaning of Paul's "exception" in 1 Corinthians 7:15.

These issues have been the hub of theological debate through the centuries, giving rise to five major views.

1. The Patristic (or early Church Fathers) view
2. The Erasmian (or traditional Protestant) view
3. The Preteritive (or Augustinian) view
4. The Betrothal (or engagement) view
5. The Consanguinity (or unlawful marriages) view

It should be pointed out that some of these views are little heard of today outside of scholarly circles, while others have received more attention by the general public through popular books on the home and family that defend those positions.

The popularity of a view is not a criterion for determining its accuracy, however. It is well to note that a large number of serious scholars reject as untenable the most common and pop-ular view of the five, the only one that allows for remarriage. While none of the views is without problems, it is interesting that recent scholarship is coming down on the side of a much stricter approach to the question. We will in the remainder of this chapter state each view briefly and then in the next chapter explain more fully their arguments.

The Patristic View

Careful research through the hundreds of manuscripts written by church leaders of the first five centuries has revealed that with only one exception (Ambrosiaster, a fourth-century Latin writer), the Church Fathers were unanimous in their under-standing that Christ and Paul taught that if one were to suffer the misfortune of divorce, remarriage was not permitted, re-gardless of the cause.[10]

This remained the standard view of the church until the sixteenth century when Erasmus suggested a different idea that was taken over by Protestant theologians.[11] In the Patristic view, the only reasonable explanation for the disciples' reaction to Christ's words in Matthew 19:10 was that Christ was not following the arguments of the rabbinical schools of either Hillel (divorce and remarriage allowed for any trivial reason) or Sham-mai (divorce and remarriage allowed in cases of adultery), but was presenting an entirely revolutionary concept—that divorce is sinful and not according to God's plan; but if divorce were to take place, remarriage was forbidden. Great weight was given to the word order of Matthew 19:9 which, the Fathers held, forbade remarriage even when immorality was involved.

The Erasmian View

This view of the divorce/remarriage issue is by far the most widely accepted today among Protestants. It holds that Christ's words in Matthew 19:9 allowed divorce in the case of adultery; and, since in Jewish marriage contracts the granting of divorce always implied the right to remarry, He also was permitting the innocent party to remarry. Most of those who take this position also say that Paul further expanded this concept by allowing for divorce and remarriage in the case of the willful desertion on the part of the person's partner. Many even go further by allowing divorce and remarriage to take place for a variety of reasons—irreconcilable differences, mental promiscuity, mistreatment, etc.

At the beginning of the Reformation, the classical humanist Desiderius Erasmus suggested this interpretation and it is defended by the modern reformed scholar John Murray.[12] Erasmus was a contemporary of Luther who influenced Luther's thinking on a number of issues but eventually broke with the reformers.

It is curious that though Erasmus was essentially regarded as a heretic by his contemporaries, the Reformation writers were greatly influenced by his doctrine of divorce and remarriage. Since most evangelical literature has in turn been influenced by the reformers and, subsequently by the Westminster Confession, his view is widely held among evangelicals today.

The Preteritive View
This view is not given a great deal of consideration by other than serious scholars, due to its quite complicated exegesis which makes it difficult to explain to the English reader. We are indebted to Bill Heth, who has done extensive research in the subject, for clarifying this view for us.

Simply stated, the Preteritive view, promoted by Augustine, holds that the Pharisees were trying to trick Jesus into entering a debate between the liberal school of Hillel and the more conservative school of Shammai, but Christ did not take the bait. Instead He deftly avoided the issue until He was in private with His disciples, where He clarified His meaning (Mark 10:10-12).

The controversy was over the meaning of Deuteronomy 24:1,

"some indecency." They asked Christ to comment. The Augustinian view holds that Christ's words "except for immorality" were actually a preterition (a passing over) which bypassed their question altogether. Christ said, "And I say to you, whoever divorces his wife [setting aside the issue of the meaning of 'some indecency'] and marries another woman commits adultery." Then when they were alone with Christ in the house, and the disciples were pressing Him to settle the dispute, He said, "Whoever divorces his wife and marries another woman commits adultery against her" (Mark 10:11).

This seems to cover the cultural possibility that in Roman culture divorce was required in the case of adultery and Christ was in such a case forbidding remarriage. Because the evidence in support of Augustine's opinion is stronger than generally recognized, it is surprising it is so seldom discussed as a possibility in the plethora of popular books on this subject.

The Betrothal View

This view claims that Christ's exception clause (Matthew 19:9) allowed for the breaking of an engagement in the case of a violation of the betrothal terms by the immorality of one party, previous to consummating the actual marriage.

The arguments in favor of this position have merit. When one understands the binding nature of betrothal in the time of Christ, and the clear recognition of the need for a "divorce" to break the engagement (as illustrated by Mary and Joseph in Matthew 1:18-20), one can readily see that such an interpretation is possible. Since engaged couples referred to their fiances as "husband" or "wife," it is said that for Christ to not address Himself to this possibility would have opened the way to misunderstanding and shut the door on even the breaking of an engagement. The point is made that Christ carefully chose the word "fornication" (*porneia*) to stand in contrast to "adultery" (*moicheia*). Both words speak of sexual unfaithfulness, the former to premarital unfaithfulness and the second to marital unfaithfulness.

The Betrothal view, held by a number of evangelical scholars, has much to commend it.

The Consanguinity View

This view, defended admirably in Carl Laney's book, *The Divorce Myth,* holds that Christ used the word *porneia* in the specialized sense of the prohibited degrees of consanguinity and affinity in Leviticus 18:6-18.[13] Hence a divorce would be allowed in the extraordinary circumstance of being married to a near relative. Apart from this circumstance, neither divorce nor remarriage would be permitted. There is considerable support for this view in Acts 15:20, 29 and 1 Corinthians 5:1 and in the Dead Sea Scrolls.

The arguments in favor of the Consanguinity view are strong enough that those dealing with the divorce/remarriage problem feel some need to discuss them. But it is disappointing to see them cast the view off as untenable with only cursory comments since, in fact, it has wide support in scholarly circles. While it is not without its difficulties (as is true of all five positions), it does have much to commend it.

With divorce being the problem it is in our day, it is imperative that we look for the view that is not just the most palatable to our age, but the one that is most true to God's ideal, most consistent with God's character, and which fits most accurately all biblical data on the subject.

The Question of Remarriage

Before concluding this survey, it may be helpful to summarize what each of these views says about remarriage.

1. The Patristic view disallows remarriage even though a divorce has occurred. This was the Lord's teaching as well as the Apostle Paul's understanding of His teaching. Only two alternatives exist: be reconciled or remain unmarried (1 Corinthians 7:11).

2. The Erasmian view, which allows for divorce in cases of

adultery or desertion (other reasons are also added today), permits the "innocent" party to remarry without any question. If the divorce is legitimate, this grants freedom to the offended party to remarry.

3. The Preteritive view, while recognizing that divorce may happen, does not permit remarriage.

4. The Betrothal view concerns giving a bill of divorce during the period of engagement before the marriage is consummated in case of premarital unchastity. Therefore, there never was a first marriage, only an engagement. Thus the offended party could enter into a second engagement which, when consummated, would be the first marriage.

5. The Consanguinity view, though recognizing that divorce may have to be instituted in cases of unlawful marriages, considers remarriage of such persons contrary to both Christ's and Paul's teachings. It also holds that in the case of a lawful marriage, divorce is forbidden and the remarriage of a divorced person is never permitted.

Observe that only the Erasmian view permits remarriage. This may account for its popularity today! But it should be noted that even if immorality justifies divorce, the texts in question actually do not justify remarriage. The modernization of the Erasmian view seems to assume that remarriage is automatically permitted if divorce occurs for the permitted reason(s). But this is an exegetical leap of faith!

Today a strained exegesis of 1 Corinthians 7:15 is used to justify remarriage in cases of desertion of the believing partner by the unbelieving mate. Paul says that the believer "is not under bondage" in such cases. This is understood by modern Erasmians as meaning that the believer is free to remarry. Checking a number of commentaries on this verse, we found that the vast majority agreed that the meaning is that the believer is not bound to keep the marriage together and may have to accept separation if the unbeliever departs. As one suggested, the believing partner was not bound to chase the unbeliever all over the Roman Empire if the unbeliever chose to leave!

Of course, commentators can be wrong; but the burden of proof is certainly on those who say that the phrase frees the believer to remarry. Paul did not even discuss remarriage in that chapter until the end (v. 39), and then only in the case of the widowed. Clearly the Christian must dare to stand against the tide of easy divorce.

Divorce took the spotlight in an unprecedented way in the spring of 1971 when filming began on a nine-part documentary, *An American Family.* The series featured a "Typical American Family," the William C. Loud family from Santa Barbara, California, distilling seven months of their life into twelve hours of televised drama. The real shock came when, in the presence of ten million viewers, Pat Loud told her husband of twenty years to move out.

Tragically, such family scenes are all too typical. But what is typical for the society in which we live cannot be typical for believers in Christ. We are to live by the standards of truth taught in the Bible.

FOOTNOTES

1. "The Broken Family: Divorce U.S. Style," *Newsweek,* March 12, 1973, p. 47.

2. Donald B. Louria, "The American Family—A Dim Future," *Current Research on Marriage, Families, and Divorce,* (New York: Atcom, Inc., 1979), p. 2.

3. Albert Ellis, quoted by J. Allan Petersen, *Reasons for Marriage Failure,* Family & Marriage Success Series, Family Concern, Inc., (Omaha, Nebraska, 1972), p. 3.

4. Norman Lobsenz and Clark W. Blackburn, "Hidden Meanings of Money in Marriage," *Reader's Digest,* March 1969, p. 142.

5. Bishop R.C. Trench in his *Synonyms of the New Testament* points out that the Greek word here which means "one who cannot be persuaded to enter into a covenant" can also mean "untrue to one's promise." (Marshalltown, Del.: The National Foundation for Christian Education).

6. Elton Trueblood, *The Incendiary Fellowship,* (New York: Harper & Row, 1978).

7. James Dobson, *Straight Talk to Men and Their Wives,* (Waco, Texas: Word Books, 1981), p. 92.

8. Dwight Hervey Small, "Divorce and Remarriage—A Fresh Biblical Perspective," *Theology, News and Notes,* March 1976.

9. Mary LaGrand Bouma, *Divorce in the Parsonage,* (Minneapolis: Bethany Fellowship, 1979), p. 147.

10. Gordon Wenham, "The Biblical Way of Marriage and Divorce, #3, New Testament Teaching," *Third Way* (London), November 17, 1977.

11. Bill Heth, *An Analysis and Critique of the Evangelical Protestant View of Divorce and Remarriage,* Th.M. Thesis, Dallas Theological Seminary, May 1982, p. 11 of supplement.

12. John Murray, *Divorce,* (Phillipsburg, N.J.: Presbyterian and Reformed Publishing Company, 1961), pp. 99-103.

13. J. Carl Laney, *The Divorce Myth,* (Minneapolis: Bethany House Publishers, 1981), pp. 71-78.

5 VIEWS OF THE DIVORCE QUESTION

These five views do not discuss the higher critical views which are untenable for those who hold to an inerrant Scripture.

VIEW	Deuteronomy 24:1-4	Matthew 5:31-32
1. PATRISTIC (Early Church Fathers) VIEW	Emphasis on "defiled" — vs. 4. What defiled her? Second marriage = adultery. The fact that she was "put away" by husband did not assume right to remarry.	Christ teaching a higher law than Moses allowed. Divorce certificate must be given. Christ allowed divorce for sexual sin, but grammar and syntax forbid remarriage.
2. ERASMIAN (Reformed or Traditional Protestant) VIEW	Emphasis on "some un-cleanness" — vs. 1. Same interpretation as Shammai. Adultery = grounds for divorce = right to remarry is assumed.	Divorce allowed in case of adultery. Remarriage permitted.
3. Preteritive (Augustinian or No Comment) VIEW	Not discussed because not important to argument.	The phrase "except for" is a preterition; commonly known that debate was over meaning of "some uncleanness." Christ set that aside.
4. BETROTHAL (Engage-ment) VIEW	Term "husband" and "wife" can refer to engaged couple (Deut. 22:23, 24; 2 Sam. 3:14; Matt. 1:18-25). Therefore — "some un-cleanness" is marriage test (Num. 5:11-30). If she marries she cannot return to former fiance.	"Except for fornication" means a breach of marriage contract before marriage is consummated. An engage-ment can be broken, a mar-riage cannot. Remarriage forbidden.
5. CONSANGUIN-ITY (Unlawful Marriages) VIEW	Moses acknowledges that divorce happens and it is regulated but not encouraged. Restriction placed on remarriage to original partner if there is a marriage in between.	"Except for unchastity" refers to incest laws of Leviticus 18. Note Acts 15 where same word is used in this regard.

Matthew 19:1-12	MEANING OF PORNEIA	EUNUCH SAYING	Mark 10:1-2
Christ says that God's best is monogamy. Divorce was a concession to hard hearts. Roman law might require a divorce in case of adultery. Remarriage expressly forbidden.	Adultery	Proof that remarriage is forbidden.	God's best is monogamy. Divorce is concession to hard hearts. Remarriage expressly forbidden.
Christ says that God's best is monogamy. Divorce was a concession to hard hearts. Divorce permitted to innocent party in case of adultery. Remarriage allowed to innocent party.	Adultery	Not germane to context.	God's best is monogamy. Divorce is concession to hard hearts. No need to repeat exception clause since Matthew had it.
Christ says that God's best is monogamy. Divorce was a concession to hard hearts. Exception clause a preterition. Christ refused to comment, taught the whole picture to disciples privately. Remarriage forbidden.	"Some unclean-ness" — (Deut. 24).	Proof that remarriage is forbidden, private saying.	God's best is monogamy. Divorce is concession to hard hearts. Private saying holds precedence.
Christ says that God's best is monogamy. Divorce was a concession to hard hearts. Exception clause refers to breaking of betrothal covenant. Remarriage forbidden after divorce from fully consummated marriage.	Sexual promiscuity before marriage.	Proof that remarriage is forbidden.	God's best is monogamy. Divorce is concession to hard hearts; to Roman readers; no need to refer to Jewish betrothal law.
Christ says that God's best is monogamy. Divorce was a concession to hard hearts. Divorce allowed in case of next of kin marriages. Remarriage forbidden.	Incestuous marriage.	Proof that remarriage is forbidden.	God's best is monogamy. Divorce is concession to hard hearts. Exception clause would be misunderstood by Roman readers.

VIEW	Luke 16:18	1 Corinthians 7:10-16	CONCLUSION
1. PATRISTIC (Early Church Fathers) VIEW	Remarriage was forbidden.	Paul understood Christ's words to leave only two alternatives, reconciliation or remaining single. No remarriage permitted.	Divorce may sometimes happen; remarriage is never permitted and is clearly contrary to Scripture.
2. ERASMIAN (Reformed or Traditional Protestant) VIEW	No need to repeat exception since Matthew said it.	Paul added another legitimate cause for divorce: desertion. Remarriage allowed.	Divorce allowed for adultery or desertion; remarriage permitted.
3. Preteritive (Augustinian or No Comment) VIEW	Remarriage was forbidden.	Paul understood Christ's words to leave only two alternatives, reconciliation or remaining single. No remarriage permitted.	Divorce may sometimes happen; remarriage is never permitted and is clearly contrary to Scripture.
4. BETROTHAL (Engagement) VIEW	Remarriage was forbidden; use of *pornéia* here would be misunderstood by Greek readers.	Paul understood Christ's words to leave only two alternatives, reconciliation or remaining single. No remarriage permitted.	Divorce (breaking the engagement) may sometimes happen; remarriage is not an issue because a first marriage was never consummated.
5. CONSAN- GUINITY (Unlawful Marriages) VIEW	Remarriage was forbidden; use of *pornéia* here would be misunderstood by Greek readers.	Paul understood Christ's words to leave only two alternatives, reconciliation or remaining single. No remarriage permitted.	Divorce may sometimes happen; remarriage is never permitted and is clearly contrary to Scripture.

9

Probing the
Views on Divorce

"Methodists Favor U.S. Divorce Law," was the headline in the *Sacramento Union*. And below it, "Ministers to refuse to marry persons divorced." The article read:

> The Southern California Methodist Conference went on record today in the closing session as favoring a federal divorce law and urging that ministers refuse to marry divorced persons. According to the report of the Committee on Marriage and Divorce, "Divorce is to the home what fuse is to the dynamite."
> The date of the article—October 8, 1912.

As recently as thirty years ago, divorces were considered abnormal, marriage vows were taken seriously, and debate over the divorce/remarriage issue was limited to theological conferences. Even the non-Christian populace held strict standards on these matters. Corporations often would fire executives whose marriages were breaking up. People refused to elect government officials who had divorce in their background.

The Christian community, recognizing that sinners (including divorcees) are forgiven, redeemed, and reconciled to God through Jesus Christ, welcomed people into the church regardless of their past. But if a person who professed to be a believer initiated a divorce or if a divorcee wanted to remarry, it was open scandal. If the average believer was aware of the "exception clause" and the interpretation of the reformers, he seldom exercised his option. Divorce among believers was practically unheard of.

With modern times bringing a "new morality" and divorce/remarriage becoming an accepted lifestyle among the general populace, the church has allowed its standards to slip. As in the Arab proverb, the camel stuck its nose inside the tent and soon took over.

A greater number of lay people (especially women) are reading more than ever before. Three decades ago, few Christian books were written for the person in the pew, and books on such practical subjects as marriage and divorce were rare. Today, bookstores are filled with books on all aspects of family life. As a more educated and sophisticated Christian public has discovered that there is no agreement among theologians on the divorce/remarriage issue, many people have clamored after books that justify what they privately have wanted to do for a long time. Books addressing the issue from the Erasmian view are best-sellers. The resulting problem is enormous. One church in Southern California has over two hundred couples in it; yet only four of those couples are married to their original mates!

Almost all evangelical theologians would agree that divorce is not God's plan, that remarriage at best is a concession to sinful man, that God hates divorce, and that God's original design at Creation was monogamy. But we have built a doctrine on a single phrase of Scripture—"except for fornication" (KJV), the meaning of which is certainly debatable. Let's examine more closely the five views mentioned in the previous chapter and see if we can determine where the weight of evidence lies.

The Patristic View

In a series of three articles in a British publication, *Third Way*, Gordon Wenham examines "The Biblical View of Marriage and Divorce."[1] In the first article he considers the cultural background for divorce and remarriage in all the ancient world, showing that while society did allow divorce, it was both expensive and rare. In his second article he examines the Old Testament teaching on this subject, dealing with the bride-money (or dowry) and other social customs. Here he raises a very important point and one largely ignored by most books on divorce.

It is an idea that centers around Deuteronomy 24:1-4 and is dealt with more thoroughly by other scholars.[2] The rabbinical school of Hillel focused its attention on the fact that a husband finds "some indecency" in the wife. The question asked was, "What is some indecency?" The answer? Burning her husband's dinner, talking with another man, or almost anything else. If the husband was displeased, he had grounds for divorce. It was the ancient equivalent to no-fault divorce.

To counter the liberal view, the school of Shammai rose up in protest. " 'Some uncleanness' means adultery and only adultery," it taught. The controversy raged and prompted the question to the Lord Jesus in Matthew 19 and Mark 10. When they posed the question, "Is it lawful for a man to divorce his wife for any cause at all?" (Matthew 19:3) the Pharisees were asking Jesus to confirm or deny Hillel's popular position. Instead, Christ appealed to God's original design of monogamous marriage. When the Pharisees reminded Him of the provision for divorce in the Mosaic Law, Christ made clear that "permission" was given because of hardness of man's heart but was not God's desire.

The issue Wenham and others raise is whether the emphasis of the passage is on "some indecency" or whether it more properly should be on Matthew 19:4 and on the fact that the former wife is "defiled" and cannot return to her first husband even if the second husband dies.

The emphasis of the passage forbids the husband from taking the original wife back, regardless of the cause of the first divorce, when there has been a second marriage in between. Why would this be so even if the second husband dies? Because the wife is actually "defiled" by the second marriage, it is an "abomination before the Lord" and there is danger of bringing "sin on the land" (Deuteronomy 24:4). To shed light on the meaning of defilement, Wenham comments on Leviticus 18:

> A spouse's relationship with the family is not terminated by death of the partner who belonged to it by birth nor is it ended by divorce. As far as her husband's family is concerned, the divorced wife still belongs to them and thus may not marry anyone closely related to her husband ... the horizontal relationships are as enduring as the vertical ones. It thus seems to imply that to seek a divorce is to try and break a relationship with one's wife that cannot really be broken."[3]

Thus, for a woman to return to her original partner would be a kind of incest and thus forbidden. This would make Deuteronomy 24:1-4 not a permission for divorce, as Hillel and Shammai assumed, but merely an acknowledgment that divorce did happen. However, if there was a subsequent remarriage, there could be no return to one's former partner under any circumstances.

This, in part, leads Wenham to conclude: "It is ... intrinsically probable that the Patristic interpretation ... is the correct one."[4]

The Patristic view interprets Matthew 19:9 as forbidding remarriage regardless of the cause of divorce. This view is seen in writings of church leaders during the first five centuries and was the official position of the church until the sixteenth century.

The Fathers usually understood "except for unchastity" to mean that divorce was allowable in the case of adultery, but remarriage was expressly forbidden. They did not believe that

Paul in 1 Corinthians 7, "allowed the believing, deserted spouse to remarry."[5]

There is considerable grammatical support for this interpretation because the location of the exception clause serves only to modify the immediate phrase in which it is found, not the following phrase concerning remarriage. The Church Fathers believed that if a sexual sin occurred, divorce was permitted but remarriage was not; and that if both divorce and remarriage occurred, adultery had been committed. If the exception clause were found at the beginning of the verse, it would require divorce in the case of adultery. If it were placed after both verbs, "put away" and "marries," it would allow both divorce and remarriage. But where it is in the verse, it allows divorce if *porneia* has occurred, but does not allow for remarriage. This then is consistent with the interpretation of Deuteronomy 24:1-4 suggested above. For one to remarry after divorce is to commit adultery and be defiled. It is also consistent with the fact that Luke 16 and Mark 10 record Christ forbidding remarriage, without an exception.

An updating of the Patristic view relates the exception clause in Matthew to the fact that for the Jewish people, adultery was first and foremost a sin against God. This is why it demanded a punishment by the community. The husband could not pardon his wife on his own. In contrast, Roman law viewed adultery as a matter of private family law. This is why only Matthew, whose readers were largely Jewish, includes the exception clause.

How would Matthew's readers have understood it? It is suggested that they would understand Jesus to be saying that He would not hold the disciples guilty of violating His absolute prohibition of divorce if they found themselves in a situation where a mate had committed adultery, which would force them to institute a divorce. The divorce would be necessitated only by the mores of the Jewish community which would require the action because of the community effect of the sin of adultery in Judaism. In such a case the Lord was saying He would

understand why a divorce was necessary. This in no way constitutes a universal ground for divorce, because the circumstances
could not be duplicated today. Neither, of course, does it permit
remarriage. Indeed, Matthew 19:1-12 makes it very clear that
a remarriage would involve committing adultery.[6]

The Erasmian View

This view, by far the most popular among evangelicals today,
seems on the surface to be the simplest to understand and,
because of its wide acceptance, to be the correct one. However,
when it is examined thoroughly, it is not so clearly conclusive.
And since this is the only view of the five that allows for remarriage after divorce, it is crucial that it be examined carefully.

The logic of the reformers that rose from Erasmus's deep
human concern for the individual was this. If one partner committed adultery, he would, according to Old Testament law, be
stoned to death. Therefore, it was assumed that the adulterous
partner was "as dead in God's sight," thus freeing the "innocent" party to remarry. This, said the reformers, was behind
Jesus' exception clause, and thus the innocent party was free
to divorce and remarry whenever immorality was involved.

This idea has been espoused from Luther to the present day.
E.J. Ehrlich calls it "legal fiction"[7] since it assumes the adulter-
er should be treated "as if he were dead."[8] Because of the
obvious absurdity of "legal fiction," many evangelical writers
today do not follow that idea, but it is still heard on occasion.
The fact is, the person is still very much alive, and a supposed
"death" does not negate the marriage. Nevertheless, this is the
kind of reasoning which popularized the Erasmian doctrine.

Erasmus, a contemporary of Martin Luther, was considered
a friend of the Reformation because he spoke out against the
abuses of power in the Catholic Church. Luther broke with him,
however, because of Erasmus's heretical ideas and his weak
view on justification by faith. But for some reason, Luther
favored his ideas on divorce and remarriage, thus rejecting the
teaching and practice of the early church.

Erasmus allowed for divorce and remarriage of the innocent party in cases of adultery or desertion. Since he developed his doctrine on a subjective base rather than a grammatical or exegetical one, the reformers began with an Erasmian presupposition and tried to prove it exegetically. They began by demonstrating from the Old Testament that divorce was sometimes allowed, failing to mention that so were polygamy and slavery. Like the Pharisees of Jesus' time, the reformers referred to the "bill of divorce" mentioned in Deuteronomy 24, often ignoring that Christ said it was allowed because of hardness of heart. From an ancient divorce document (found in the Encyclopedia Judaica),[9] they tried to prove that when divorce was permitted, remarriage always was a live option.

Further, they assumed that *porneia* (fornication) equals *moicheia* (adultery), a matter to be discussed later. Then ignoring the force of word order in Christ's statement in Matthew 19:9, they concluded that the "innocent party" (the one who did not commit adultery) was free to remarry. Based on the above assumptions, they declared that although Mark and Luke omitted the "exception clause," because Matthew stated it, it should automatically be implied in the Mark and Luke texts. This, in spite of the fact that many scholars believe Mark was written first, which would mean that the early readers of Mark did not have access to Matthew and the exception clause.

They drew the same conclusions about Paul's words in 1 Corinthians 7:10-11:

> But to the married I give instructions, not I, but the Lord, [he bases this on the words of Jesus in Matthew 5, 19; Mark 10; and Luke 16] that the wife should not leave her husband (but if she does leave, let her remain unmarried, or else be reconciled to her husband), and that the husband should not send his wife away.

Paul did not express an exception at all, but the Erasmian view says it is implied. One writer supports this opinion by saying, "For a thing to be true, God has only to say it once."[10] Of course, that is true, and also irrelevent to this point. No one denies that Christ said "except for fornication." It is not a question of truth, but of harmonization with other passages. To claim that Christ's saying it once allows us to imply the exception in other statements by Christ and Paul is an unprovable conclusion. Furthermore, one should consider Augustine's rule of interpretation in the Synoptics: Start with what is clear in Mark and Luke to understand what is ambiguous in Matthew, since Matthew is an inherently Jewish Gospel.[11]

Finally, the Erasmian view, having opened up a door to an exception in Jesus' teaching, swings it wide open to find another exception in 1 Corinthians 7. Paul, they say, allows divorce and remarriage in the case of an unbeliever deserting a believing partner. This, in spite of the fact that the text is speaking of separation or desertion, and of divorce only by implication. It is completely silent on the subject of remarriage. This then forces those of the Erasmian persuasion to interpret the sentence, "The brother or the sister is not under bondage in such cases," as giving blanket permission for remarriage. The text does not say that. In fact, it seems to contradict it by the very next phrase: "But God has called us to peace." The Greek word translated in the KJV in Acts 7:26, "set them at one again," denotes the strongest idea of unity, wholeness, and reconciliation. If God indeed calls the believing partner to reconciliation, then Paul remained consistent with what he told the Christian couple in 1 Corinthians 7:11; namely, that if separation occurs, the only two options are to remain unmarried or be reconciled. This too is in line with what Paul relates in 1 Corinthians 7:39: "A wife is bound as long as her husband lives; but if her husband is dead, she is free to be married to whom she wishes, only in the Lord." It is also harmonious with the illustration in Romans 7:2-3:

For the married woman is bound by law to her husband while he is living; but if her husband dies, she is released from the law concerning the husband. So then if, while her husband is living, she is joined to another man, she shall be called an adulteress; but if her husband dies, she is free from the law, so that she is not an adulteress, though she is joined to another man.

We believe that the Erasmian view is weak in its foundation and shaky in its superstructure. Proponents of the view work diligently to convince the evangelical public that only a few reputable scholars hold dissenting views. That simply is not true.

Charles Hodge, in his Commentary on First Corinthians, comments on chapter 7 by saying:

The uniform doctrine of the New Testament is that marriage is a contract for life, between one man and one woman, indissoluble by the will of the parties or by any human authority; but that the death of either party leaves the survivor free to contract another marriage.[12]

A.T. Robertson and A. Plummer say, "All that 'he is not bound' clearly means is that he or she need not feel so bound by Christ's prohibition of divorce as to be afraid to depart when the heathen partner insists on separation."[13]

S. Lewis Johnson in the Wycliffe Bible Commentary writes:

Nothing is said about a second marriage for the believer; it is vain to put words in Paul's mouth when he is silent. It is true that the verb "to depart" in the middle voice (it is middle in this verse) was almost a technical term for divorce in the papyri (M.M. pp. 695-696). This, however, really proves nothing here.[14]

Geoffrey Bromiley, in his delightful theology of marriage entitled *God and Marriage,* states, "The door of reconciliation must be left open. Implicitly if not explicitly, remarriage by either partner in the case of separation is viewed as adultery."[15] He later says:

> Believers do not ... have to accept the new and nonbiblical situation that is thrust upon them and abandon their own faithfulness to the covenantal marriage. A readiness for reconciliation may be one-sided, as God was with Israel, but so long as the door stays open a response can still come from the other side. ... If the readiness for reconciliation makes a stern demand, this, after all, is what being a disciple is all about.[16]

The Preteritive View

The word *preteritive* simply means "to bypass." When used to label a view of the exception clause, it means that Christ bypassed the entire discussion of whether or not *porneia* was a legitimate reason for divorce. The rabbinical school of Shammai taught that "some uncleanness" of Deuteronomy 24 meant adultery, while the school of Hillel interpreted it to mean "any cause at all." So obviously both schools did teach that adultery could be a ground for divorce.

The Preteritive view holds that Christ, when commenting on Deuteronomy 24 in Matthew 5:32 and 19:9, deliberately bypassed the question of *porneia* as a possible ground for divorce. Both rabbinic schools contended that "some uncleanness" meant at least *porneia*. Christ would not be sidetracked to discuss that point lest His main point be lost. And His main point took His hearers back to God's original intention for marriage, as revealed in Genesis 1 and 2 which did not allow for divorce at all.

The proponents of this view point out that it was not at all unusual for Christ to bypass the argument of opponents and kibitzers who sought to trick Him or sidetrack His message from the main point. Matthew 21:23-27 furnishes a classic example of the Lord's method. The chief priests and elders tried to trap Jesus by asking, "By what authority are You doing these things, and who gave You this authority?" (v. 23) Instead of responding to the question of His authority, the Lord countered with another question which threw the leaders into a dilemma so that they chose not to answer. Then Christ likewise refused to tell them by what authority He was acting. In such situations the Lord would often answer cryptically, while at the same time enticing those who really wanted an answer to quiz Him later.

In Matthew 5:32 the word translated "except" may well be translated "setting aside" or "apart from." The only other two places in the New Testament where the word is used support this. In Acts 26:29 Paul said that he desired King Agrippa and the others in the audience who heard him to become as he was "apart from" his chains. In 2 Corinthians 11:23-27 Paul described the physical hardships he had endured for the Gospel. Then he said that "apart from" those external hardships he was constantly under the daily burden of his deep concern for the welfare of the churches (v. 28). Using this idea in Matthew 5:32 Christ's meaning would be this: "Moses said that whoever puts away his wife should give her a bill of divorce; but I say that whoever puts away his wife causes her to commit adultery, and I say this 'apart from' entering into any discussion of *porneia.*"

In Matthew 19:9 the phrase includes a negative (*mē*), a preposition (*epi*), and the noun *porneia*. The preposition translated "for" in our English versions is nowhere else translated that way in Matthew. Actually, with a negative, it should be translated "not on the grounds or basis of *porneia.*" According to the Preteritive view, this means that "*porneia* is not involved." Again Christ was bypassing the question of *porneia*. Augustine translated this, "without the cause of immorality."[17]

Further, one would not expect the disciples' reaction to be what it was if the Lord had allowed *porneia* to be a legitimate ground for divorce. They replied that if what He had said was true, it was better not to marry. To this Jesus replied:

> "Not all men can accept this statement, but only those to whom it has been given. For there are eunuchs who were born that way from their mother's womb; and there are eunuchs who were made eunuchs by men, and there are also eunuchs who made themselves eunuchs for the sake of the kingdom of heaven.

He who is able to accept this, let him accept it" (Matthew 19:11-12).

That this so-called "eunuch saying" is for the committed disciple is indicated by the twice-used statement, "He who is able to accept this, let him accept it." This does not imply that the teaching on the indissolubility of marriage is not a standard at all, but rather that it must be a standard disciples live up to.

Incidentally, the Erasmians tend to ignore the eunuch saying. Most of them fail to comment on it in any detail, and when questioned about it simply pass it off as not germane to the context. However, the importance of this saying should not be underestimated.

Clearly the disciples were expressing considerable surprise at the stringent standard which Christ had set forth. Then in what seems to have been a private clarification session with the disciples, Christ pointed out, "For God's sake some people may have to forego marriage, some may have to put it in a new perspective, and some who have broken their marriages may have to refrain from remarriage."[18]

The Betrothal View

This view, held by a number of competent scholars, has much to commend it. Proponents of this view point out that in several passages of Scripture (Galatians 5:19; Hebrews 13:4; and especially Matthew 15:19 and Mark 7:21), fornication is clearly distinguished from adultery. Their conclusion is that fornication is a sexual relationship before marriage. Adultery is an illicit sexual relationship after marriage.

The betrothal arrangement in Israel was considered totally binding upon the betrothed partners. Alfred Edersheim says:

> From the moment of betrothal both parties were regarded, and treated by law (as to inheritance, adultery, need of formal divorce), as if they had been actually married, except as regarded their living together."[19]

There are two passages that seem to support this thesis. One is Matthew 1:19, where Joseph was contemplating his option of putting Mary "away privately" after he discovered she was "with child." It was obvious to him that although he had not touched her sexually, someone must have; therefore, formal divorce was necessary to nullify the engagement. Though the word *fornication* is not specifically used, this was the assumed sin. This comes into focus again in John 8:41 where the Pharisees' denial of being "born of fornication" (*porneia*) may indicate that they suspected that He was conceived before Mary and Joseph were married.

Critics of this view are quick to point out that it is marriage, not engagement, that is in view in Matthew 5 and 19. But since the terms "husband," "wife" (see Deuteronomy 22:23, 24; 2 Samuel 3:14; Matthew 1:18-25), and "put away" as well as "bill of divorcement" were used for an engaged couple without a fully consummated marriage, could not Christ have covered just such an exigency by that simple phrase? The omission of the exception in Mark and Luke would be clearly because their Gentile readers would not understand *porneia* to have this special meaning, as would the Jewish readers of Matthew.

Perhaps the most scholarly presentation of the Betrothal view available to English readers is the work by Abel Isaksson entitled *Marriage and Ministry in the New Temple*. In this doctoral thesis presented originally to the University of Uppsala in Sweden, Isaksson concludes,

> Linguistically speaking, the most probable meaning of *porneia*, when used in a statement of a legal nature about a married woman's crime, is undoubtedly premarital unchastity. If we interpret *porneia* in the clause in Matthew as referring to premarital unchastity and consider this clause in terms of the historical background, it does not appear to be a strange and hardly comprehensible exception from the rule about the absolute indissolubility of marriage. It is not a question of an exception from the rule that a consummated marriage is indissoluble. The word

divorce is used even when a man divorces his wife because of her premarital unchastity.[20]

This view has good evidence to support it.

The Consanguinity View

The Consanguinity (or unlawful marriage) view is favored by a number of writers, including the authors of this book. It is often passed by as untenable by those of the Erasmian persuasion. But upon careful examination, it seems to enjoy a number of advantages over some of the other views and is, among scholars, the most defended.

As mentioned in the Betrothal view, it is important to note that Scripture sometimes distinguishes between adultery and fornication. In fact, there is no clear New Testament reference that equates adultery with fornication, and the extrabiblical references given to make such an equation are by no means conclusive.[21] Sometimes the term *porneia* may include adultery in certain contexts and certainly does refer to various sexual aberrations in the Greek and Roman world. However, when one considers the distinctive Jewishness of Matthew's Gospel he must ask the question, "What did *porneia* mean to a first-century Jew?" Is there a clear reference in Scripture where the word in question meant something other than adultery or the less specific "general immorality?" If there is such a text, should it not have bearing on our understanding of Matthew's exception clause?

There is such a text, Acts 15:20, 29. The setting is the council in Jerusalem. The question before the group was whether or not circumcision for Gentiles was necessary for their salvation. The answer was a resounding no. It was not necessary to trouble the Gentiles who had turned to the Lord about circumcision (Acts 15:19).

But, James added, in the interest of harmony between Jewish and Gentile believers, they would ask Gentile believers to abstain from certain practices which were perfectly proper for Gentile Christians to do but which gave offense to Jewish believers because of their background. The four practices James listed were proscribed by the holiness code of Leviticus 17—18.

- the eating of meat offered to idols (Leviticus 17:8-9);
- the eating of blood (Leviticus 17:10-12);
- the eating of strangled or improperly butchered animals (Leviticus 17:15; Exodus 22:31);
- sexual intercourse with close kin (Leviticus 18:1-17).

To be sure, Leviticus 18 goes on to forbid polygamy, adultery (v. 20), offering children to idols (v. 21), homosexuality (v. 22), and bestiality (v. 23). But these practices already were abhorrent to Jewish and Gentile believers alike and did not need to be included in James' letter. The curious thing in Acts 15 is that Luke in recording the event used the word *porneia* to speak of the laws of incest. Many agree that this is the most plausible explanation of this text. For example:

> The surprising combination of *porneia* with dietary regulations is due to the fact that the four prohibitions are based on Leviticus 17 and 18. *Porneia* here is marrying within the prohibited degrees which, according to the rabbis, was forbidden "on account of fornication" (Leviticus 18:6-18).[22]

F.F. Bruce in *The Acts of the Apostles* says:

> It seems strange to find an injunction against fornication coupled with food regulations. Illicit sexual relations were, however, regarded very lightly by the Greeks, and *porneia* was closely associated with several of their religious festivals. Here the word should probably be taken in a special sense of breaches of the Jewish marriage law, Leviticus 18, which was taken over by the church.[23]

This line of argument is strengthened considerably when one considers the use of *porneia* in 1 Corinthians 5:1, where there

is no question that it refers to an incestuous relationship. W.K.
Lowther Clarke wrote in 1929:

> The Apostolic Decree of Acts 15:29 promulgated a compro-
> mise. . . . Since the first three articles of the compromise are
> concerned with practices innocent enough to the Gentiles, the
> fourth must be of a similar nature. The passage in 1 Corinthians
> gives us the clue. *Porneia* here means marriage within the pro-
> hibited Levitical degrees. . . . [This] was a live issue, and *porneia*
> was the word by which it was known.
> Turning to St. Matthew, the problem we have to account for
> is the obscuring of the plain rule of St. Mark by an exception
> which seems inconsistent with the teaching of our Lord even in
> St. Matthew. If the foregoing argument holds, the reference is
> to the local Syrian problem. One exception is allowed to the
> universal rule: When a man who has married within the prohib-
> ited degrees puts away his wife, the word adultery is out of
> place. Rather the marriage is null. . . . There is no divorce, but
> causes of nullity may be recognized.[24]

Further evidence may be gleaned from Joseph Fitzmyer and
James R. Mueller who have given convincing evidence from the
Dead Sea Scrolls that the Qumran community used the Hebrew
zenut (which the LXX translates with *porneia*) to describe marriage within the prohibited degrees of Leviticus 18. Thus we
have Palestinian evidence from the first century that the word
porneia was used to describe incestuous marriages. While evidence that fornication = adultery is lacking, the evidence for
porneia referring to unlawful marriages is compelling.

When one considers that the letter from the Jerusalem Council was directed to Antioch (Acts 15:23) and that Antioch is the
most likely area to which Matthew's Gospel was written,[25] it
adds additional credibility to this view. The conclusion that can
be drawn is that Christ anticipated the possibility of unlawful
marriages and covered this exigency with the word *porneia* so
that in such a case, divorce (or nullity) was allowed. If a person
were to find himself in a next-of-kin marriage that was legal in

his culture, but inconsistent with the plan of God, divorce would be allowed; however, remarriage was expressly forbidden in any case.

Summary

In summary, all five views presented here agree on some basic points.

- God's best is monogamy and He hates divorce.
- Divorce under the law was a concession to hard hearts.
- Christ taught and upheld God's highest standard in His teaching.

The Patristic view and the Erasmian view agree that *porneia* may mean adultery. But the Erasmian view is the only one to allow remarriage after divorce. The other views, while recognizing that divorce may sometimes happen for various reasons, are unanimous in their conviction that remarriage is contrary to Scripture, and never permitted.

The eunuch saying in Matthew 19 indicates that Christ was not siding with either Hillel or Shammai but was presenting a concept revolutionary to the minds of the disciples. The Erasmian view ignores this context as irrelevant to what Christ said in the preceding verses. It also fails to explain adequately the clear teaching of Mark 10 and Luke 16, while the other four views see those texts as supporting their thesis that no remarriage is allowed. That too seems the most consistent with Paul's understanding of the meaning of Christ's words as given in 1 Corinthians 7:10-13.

The believer who suffers the misfortune of a divorce has two clear options: remain unmarried or be reconciled to one's mate. To teach anything else is inconsistent with God's standard for marriage.

FOOTNOTES

1. Gordon Wenham, *Third Way,* (London), October 20, 1977, pp. 3-5; November 3, 1977, pp. 7-9; November 17, 1977, pp. 7-9.

2. Abel Isaksson, *Marriage and Ministry in the New Temple,* Neil Tomkinson (trans.) with assistance of Jean Gray, (Lund: Gleerup; Copenhagen: Munksgaard, 1965), p. 21; Reuven Yaron, "On Divorce in Old Testament Times," *Revue Internationale des Droits de l'Antiquite,* Vol. 3, (1957), pp. 117-128, and also *Journal of Jewish Studies,* Vol. 17, (1966) "The Restoration of Marriage [Deut. 24:1-4]," pp. 1-11.

3. Gordon Wenham, *Third Way,* (London), November 3, 1977, p. 9.

4. Gordon Wenham, *Third Way,* (London), November 17, 1977, pp. 13-14.

5. Ibid., p. 7.

6. See Evald Lovestam, "Divorce and Remarriage in the New Testament," *The Jewish Law Journal,* (Leiden, Holland: Brill, 1981), pp. 47-65.

7. R. J. Ehrlich, "The Indissolubility of Marriage as a Theological Problem," *Scottish Journal of Theology,* August 1970, pp. 291-311.

8. Bill Heth, *Studia Theologica et Apologia,* "A Critique of the Evangelical Protestant View of Divorce and Remarriage," (P.O. Box 1030, Dallas, Texas, 1981), p. 23.

9. *Encyclopedia Judaica,* Vol. 6. (New York: Macmillan & Co., 1971), p. 123.

10. John MacArthur, Jr., *The Family,* (Chicago: Moody Press, 1982), p. 125.

11. Bill Heth, "An Analysis and Critique of Six Interpretations," *Jesus' Divorce Sayings,* (P.O. Box 1030, Dallas, Texas, 1982), p. 23.

12. Charles Hodge, *An Exposition of the First Epistle to the Corinthians,* (Grand Rapids: Wm. B. Eerdmans Publishing Co., Reprinted 1976), p. 133.

13. Archibald Robertson and Alfred Plummer, *A Critical and Exegetical Commentary on the First Epistle of St. Paul to the Corinthians,* 2nd ed., International Critical Commentary, (Edinburgh: T. & T. Clark, 1911), p. 143.

14. S. Lewis Johnson, Jr., *The Wycliffe Bible Commentary,* edited by Charles F. Pfeiffer, Everett F. Harrison, (Chicago: Moody Press, 1962), p. 1240.

15. Geoffrey Bromiley, *God and Marriage,* (Grand Rapids: Wm. B. Eerdmans Publishing Co., 1980), p. 63.

16. Ibid., pp. 68-69.

17. Augustine, "Adulterous Marriages," trans. by Charles T. Huegelmeyer in "Treatises on Marriage and Other Subjects," *The Fathers of the Church,* Vol. 27 (ed. by Joseph Deferrari) (New York: Fathers of the Church, 1955).

18. Geoffrey Bromiley, *God and Marriage,* p. 41.

19. Alfred Edersheim, *The Life and Times of Jesus the Messiah,* Vol. 1, (Grand Rapids: Wm. B. Eerdmans Publishing Co., 1979), p. 354.

20. Abel Isaksson, *Marriage and Ministry in the New Temple,* p. 140.

21. See Sirach 23:23; Isaksson's comment, p. 133; Hermas, Mandate 4, 1, 3-8 and Tobit 8:7.

22. G. Friedrich (ed.), *Theological Dictionary of the New Testament,* Vol. 6, (Grand Rapids: Wm. B. Eerdmans Publishing Co., 1971), pp. 592-593.

23. F.F. Bruce, *The Acts of the Apostles,* (Grand Rapids: Wm. B. Eerdmans Publishing Co., 1965), p. 300.

24. W.K. Lowther Clarke, *New Testament Problems,* (New York: Macmillan & Co., 1929), pp. 59-60.

25. B.H. Streeter, *The Four Gospels: A Study of Origins,* (London: Macmillan & Co., 1936), p. 16.

10

Happiness Is . . .

Wanda was a product of the radical 1960s, and when she met Fred, he became the boy of her dreams. Fred was four years older than Wanda's sixteen and a college dropout. She liked his free spirit and sophistication about drugs, and the exciting sexual revolution he advocated. When she ran away to get married, it was totally contrary to the wishes of her nominally Christian parents. A trip to Reno, a late night session with a justice of the peace, and Wanda's life was about to begin, or so she thought.

There is no gentle way to explain the torment of the next four years. In some people there seems to be such a fine line between professed love and intense hatred. Drugs and deep rebellion had left Fred incapable of proper moral judgments. His unkindness turned to cruelty, and cruelty to sadistic torture. Wanda was beaten, abused, and degraded in an unspeakable manner. She had a strong spirit, intent on proving she made a good choice. She stubbornly persisted in following her husband from town to town, living in filthy hotels and starving from lack of nourishment. The little money they had went for liquor.

One day in early spring Fred announced he was leaving Wanda

for another woman. Brokenhearted and weary, she had no place to turn but to her parents. They came to the tenderloin area of San Francisco to pick her up but were hardly prepared for what they found: their well-bred daughter, now with dirty fingernails and filthy, matted hair, her eyes looking at them with a vacant stare.

In the months after she had married, the Lord had done a work of grace in these parents' hearts, and now they looked on their Wanda with the love and compassion that Christ implants in one's heart. They took her home, nourished her, bathed and clothed her. A few days later in my office, God opened her heart to the Gospel of our Lord Jesus Christ. That day was Wanda's real beginning.

In the twenty-five years of my ministry, I have seldom seen a person respond to the truth of God's Word as quickly or eagerly as Wanda. She developed a voracious appetite for God's Word, and a zeal and love for Christ that one would desire for all believers. When she found out what God wanted her to do, she was willing. The life she had experienced in her four years with Fred had prepared her for that. What should she do?

With the careful guidance of a godly woman counselor, Wanda read in 1 Peter 2 concerning Christ's willingness to suffer and saw in 1 Peter 3:1, "In the same way, you wives. . . ." She then committed herself to seek reconciliation with the man who had been such a hard taskmaster. Her attitude was that of the Hebrew children in Daniel 3—God could protect her from harm; but if He didn't, she still would do what she knew was God's best (see Daniel 3:17-18). To make a long story short, months of her attempts to bring about reconciliation came to nothing. Fred went ahead with the divorce. Wanda made no demands; she did not fight it; she did what she could to prevent it, but the decree was granted. Fred married the woman he had been living with for almost a year.

What now was in store for Wanda? To many people it would seem reasonable to think that after all she had gone through, she deserved a little happiness. But nowhere in Scripture do you read that happiness on this earth is God's highest priority for believers. Dr. Lehman Strauss points out that for a divorced person to ask, "Can I remarry?" is to deal with the wrong question. What that person ought to ask is, "What is God's best for me now?"

This was Wanda's question. She was twenty-one and God had made her beautiful again. If she wanted to marry, she would have no problem finding a husband who could make up for the misery of her first marriage.

She now was being disciplined by an older woman who was trained in the skills of Titus 2:3-5. The woman gave Wanda an assignment—to study several Bible references on marriage and divorce and see if she could discern what God wanted for her. With her Bible, a list of texts, and the illuminating power of God's Holy Spirit, she began her quest for truth. Here is what she discovered.

• God intends that marriage be permanent.
• God hates divorce.
• Divorce has happened throughout history, but clearly is not God's ideal.
• A person who wants to obey God will seek reconciliation with his or her mate.
• When the divorce is final and the former mate marries, the door is closed on reconciliation.
• The Christian must not remarry unless the former mate dies.
• I should be willing to be single for the sake of Christ.

Wanda's conclusion: I purpose to commit myself to not remarry, but to use my time and energy to serve the Lord with all my heart and mind and strength. To avoid temptation, I will not date and I will find my fulfillment in the Lord Himself and in Christian fellowship. I believe it is God's will that I devote myself to warning other young people against rebellion, drugs, and disobedience. For this I am eminently qualified.

Today Wanda is doing just that. Now older and wiser herself, she is taking the principles taught in God's Word and instilling them in the minds and hearts of young girls.

What Is God's Best?

As if the incidence of first-marriage divorces is not high enough, the percentage of second-marriage divorces is increasing as well. Counselors persist in advising people to remarry after a divorce, as if this were the expected thing. But is it? Scripture makes it clear that the world with its desires will pass away, but, that "the one who does the will of God abides forever" (1 John 2:15-17). God has a better plan for our lives— "Do My will!"

Today many Christians seem to want to see how far they can go without stepping over the line and incurring the discipline of God. Yet we see few people who love Christ so much that they "abstain from every form of evil" (1 Thessalonians 5:22). Like the child who is told not to touch the hot stove, some people see how close they can come without getting burned. The average Christian flirts with sin, being careful not to go "too far." There is a need today to call believers back to the denial of self in following Christ, back to thinking first about what grieves Him and what pleases Him.

Should we not find our hope and satisfaction in Him, instead of seeking our own brand of happiness? Is He not enough? Do we really find Him so lacking that we have to go outside His will and His best to find fulfillment?

Mary Slessor of Calibar was an outstanding missionary. She is the subject of the African Queen series of children's missionary stories. Her field was in the jungles along the Calibar River in what is now Southeast Nigeria. She was already on the field when she fell in love with Charles Morrison, a missionary teacher who labored in the city. She wrote to her mission to request permission to marry:

Charles and I are very much in love and we would like to be married. Charles is a wonderful Christian, a very fine teacher. He would be a very great help in my jungle work. We hope that you will agree to our marriage and let Charles go into the jungle with me. I am ready to do what you say. I leave the whole matter in God's hands and will take from Him what He sees best for His work in Okayum. My life was laid on the altar for that people long ago, and I would not take one jot or tittle of it back. If it be for His glory and the advantage of His cause out there to let another join in it, I will be grateful. If not, I will be grateful, anyway.

That last statement is haunting—"If not, I will be grateful, anyway." Could you write that? Are you so content in God's will that, even if it runs cross-grain to the deepest desire of your heart, you gladly yield? Are you committed to God's best, no matter what it is? Christ in the Garden of Gethsemane, facing the unthinkable task of becoming the sin-bearer, said, "Not as I will, but as Thou wilt" (Matthew 26:39). He recognized that the purpose of life was not personal happiness, not fulfilling one's desires, not having one's own way, but doing God's will first, last, and always, and at any cost.

First Peter 2:23 reveals the secret of the patient suffering of Christ who "kept entrusting Himself to Him who judges righteously." Then Peter applied the same principle to suffering believers: "Therefore, let those also who suffer according to the will of God entrust their souls to a faithful Creator in doing what is right" (1 Peter 4:19).

That is what Mary Slessor did. She entrusted herself into the hands of a faithful Creator. When the letter came from her mission with a refusal, Mary Slessor believed that God had worked through the mission board to give her His answer to this question, and she accepted it. She loved Charles Morrison and wanted to marry him; and what she suffered no one will ever know. She longed to have a life's partner by her side; but having given her life to God, she felt that He must be her first love.

But Charles Morrison responded to the disappointment with bitterness that galled the very marrow of his bones. As a result he had a mental breakdown that led to his untimely death.

While modern mission boards do not exercise this level of authority over their missionaries, this incident is an illustration of how even a seemingly repressive authority can be used of God to accomplish His will in the life of a trusting soul.

Sharing God's Holiness

The *dis*appointments that God allows in our lives are simply *His* appointments. His commandments are not burdensome (1 John 5:3). His will is good, acceptable, and perfect (Romans 12:2). What may seem to us to be a hard blow comes from a loving hand of the omniscient sculptor who is conforming us to the image of Christ (Romans 8:28-29). His chastening, which from a purely human view is so rigid, so unfair, so demanding, has an eternal goal: "That we may share His holiness" (Hebrews 12:10). This discipline "seems not to be joyful, but sorrowful; yet to those who have been trained by it, afterwards it yields the peaceful fruit of righteousness" (Hebrews 12:11).

Did you see that key word, *afterwards?* Today, everyone wants the immediate. We have instant pudding, instant waffles, instant photographs, instant credit, and people look for instant happiness. This is one great deterrent to having a good marriage today. Marriage requires hard work, and many people don't want to put their energies into the labor required to understand and communicate and actively love. They hope it will just happen. They do not look beyond the temporal gains to the eternal consequences. "This world is the limit of their horizon" (Philippians 3:19, PH). They will not choose the hard way even if they know the easy way is wrong. They seem disinterested in the "afterwards."

When the Apostle Paul set out to do something, he took the long look. He had tasted the immediate and counted it all loss in order to gain Christ (Philippians 3:8). His goal was an eternal one. He had a "past" (3:6), but he put that behind him and he pressed on "toward the goal for the prize of the upward call of God in Christ Jesus" (3:13-14). He wanted God's best. He counseled the Colossian church: "If then you have been raised up with Christ, keep seeking the things above. . . . Set your mind on the things above, not on the things that are on earth" (Colossians 3:1-2).

Paul recognized the sacredness and validity of marriage; yet he declared that at least under certain circumstances, it was not wise to encumber oneself with a husband or wife (1 Corinthians 7:26). He made clear that the Christian separated from a mate has two options—to reconcile or remain unmarried (1 Corinthians 7:11).

Christ taught, "There are eunuchs who were born that way from their mother's womb; and there are eunuchs who were made eunuchs by men; and there are also eunuchs who made themselves eunuchs for the sake of the kingdom of heaven" (Matthew 19:12).

Scripture recommends that the older widows not remarry, but commit their remaining years to special service for God (1 Timothy 5:3-16). Even though God said, "It is not good for the man to be alone" (Genesis 2:18), it is also true that marriage or remarriage is not always God's best. The list of single missionaries and Christian workers who have affected many for God is almost endless. Yes, there is loneliness in the single life. Yes, there is disappointment; yes, there is a certain sense of incompleteness. But they can say with the psalmist, "I delight to do Thy will, O my God; Thy Law is within my heart" (Psalm 40:8).

In premarriage counseling, it is important that a pastor begin by encouraging the couple to test their relationship on the basis of God's best for their lives. A good way to do this is to measure the relationship by the plumbline of God's Word. They should be asked if they are willing to cancel their plans if it could be demonstrated that they are not within God's will. After all, the only real reason for two Christians to marry is because it is God's plan for them. That they want a family, that they love each other, and that they share a lot of common goals—these are peripheral to the real issue: "What does God want?" Mature Christian young people generally respond very positively to this line of questioning. But when a couple is challenged with God's best after a divorce has occurred, the fur flies. "I suppose you are going to tell me I cannot remarry!" is the typical response.

Scripture reminds us that God has called us to reconciliation—"but God has called us to peace" (1 Corinthians 7:15), that marriage establishes a one-flesh relationship, and that what God has joined together, no man should separate (Matthew 19:6).

Christ made clear that divorce was not in God's original plan (Matthew 19:8), and anyone who marries a divorced person commits adultery (Matthew 19:9; Mark 10:11; Luke 16:18; Matthew 5:32).

Is it not clear that it is not God's best for you to divorce? If you do, however, suffer such a misfortune, is it not equally clear that you only aggravate an already bad situation when you persist in seeking remarriage to a different partner? A commitment to serve God as a "eunuch for the kingdom of God's sake" is a privilege that should be cherished as a high calling of God in Christ Jesus.

If you are a divorced person, you are special. You have suffered—it hurts to lose. Maybe you contributed to the demise of your marriage; perhaps you were the innocent victim of circumstances beyond your control. Is this the end of the line? No!

In a moment of rage Moses disobeyed God and God in loving discipline told him that he would never enter the Promised Land (Numbers 20). Moses pled with God to change His mind, but the Lord said, "Enough! Speak to Me no more of this matter. . . . You shall not cross over this Jordan" (Deuteronomy 3:24-27).

Did Moses quit? No. He picked himself up from defeat, took his punishment like a man, accepted his more limited role, led Israel to victory (Numbers 20:21), sustained his intercessory ministry (Numbers 21:4-9), trained new leadership (Numbers 27:12-23), and left behind a legacy of truth to the next generation in the five sermons of Deuteronomy, all in the final months of his life. In the New Testament, he is called "faithful in all His house as a servant" (Hebrews 3:5). Yes, there was failure! Yes, there were limitations! But God is the God of the second chance.

God works with the failures of the past. Even though there may be certain restraints and limitations He places upon us, He picks up the broken pieces of our lives and lets us make a new beginning. With the Psalmist we can then testify:

> Before I was afflicted I went astray,
> But now I keep Thy Word" (Psalm 119:67).
> It is good for me that I was afflicted,
> That I may learn Thy statutes (Psalm 119:71).

Then we can pray, "Teach me Thy way, O Lord; I will walk in Thy truth" (Psalm 86:11).

> Submission to the will
> Of Him who guides me still
> Is surety of His love revealed;
> My soul shall rise above
> This world in which I move,
> I conquer only where I yield.
>
> Not what I wish to be,
> Nor where I wish to go,
> For who am I that I should choose my way?
> The Lord shall choose for me.
> 'Tis better far I know,
> So let Him bid me go or stay![1]

FOOTNOTES

1. C. Austin Miles, "Submission," *Favorites No. 3*, Singspiration Music, (Grand Rapids: Zondervan Corporation, 1951), p. 20.

11

Reconciliation

Jake had the haggard look of a beaten man. He had not slept much the last week. The fight with Ruth, her walking out, and the notification she had filed for divorce had preyed on his mind night after night. He stared across my desk with bleary eyes and said, "Pastor, I will do anything to get my wife back."

"Anything?" I asked.

"Anything!" he said emphatically.

My response was not at all what he expected. "Jake, that represents a sinful attitude!"

Tears welled up in those bloodshot eyes. "What do you mean? Sinful! Is it sinful for a man to want his wife back?"

"No, Jake," I replied, "it is not sinful for a man to want his wife back. But it is wrong to be willing to do anything to accomplish your goal. Would you turn your back on God? Would you surrender your moral standard? Would you lie or cheat or steal? The fact is that God does not want you to do 'anything' but simply begin to live in a way that pleases Him. The question is not, 'Are you willing to do anything to get your wife back?' but rather, 'Are you willing to do what God wants you to and trust Him for the results?' "

There is altogether too much bargaining with God these days. "God, if You get my mate back, I will do thus and so." We should do what God wants us to do because He is God and what He asks us to do is right, and not merely to achieve some selfish aim. The central issue in all we do is whether God is pleased.

The voice from heaven (Matthew 3:17) declared that God was "well-pleased" with Christ who claimed, "I do nothing on my own initiative. . . . I always do the things that are pleasing to Him" (John 8:28-29).

We so often are guilty of doing things on our own initiative, when actually our desires should be subjected to the will of Almighty God. Paul set an example for the Thessalonian church in this regard, "not as pleasing men, but God, who examines our hearts" (1 Thessalonians 2:4). And then He required the same of them, "You ought to walk and please God" (1 Thessalonians 4:1).

This matter of pleasing God is prerequisite to dealing with difficult interpersonal relationships. If we try to improve our relationships merely by pleasing people, we develop an agenda that confuses the priorities God has laid before us; and wrong priorities ultimately lead to wrong results. Proverbs 16:7 reminds us: "When a man's ways are pleasing to the Lord, He makes even his enemies to be at peace with him."

The best way to win a partner back is to live a life pleasing to God by centering your activity around God's priorities. This chapter contains some suggested steps.

Purpose to Get Right with God

Sin of any kind breaks fellowship with God (1 John 1). Most divorce situations involve a good many sinful attitudes, actions, and words on the part of both parties.

Jack and Jane, a Christian couple, went to divorce court. Jane had gotten sexually involved with a neighbor who was also assistant pastor at their church. The senior pastor of that church, angry about the disgrace, told Jack that since Jane had committed adultery she was apostate; therefore, Jack was free to remarry, and should do everything in his power to prevent Jane from getting the children.

Against the advice of cooler heads, Jack went to court to ruin Jane. Going to a great deal of expense, he produced all the evidence he could muster that she was an unfit mother. He himself took the stand and listed things that were unfair and bordered on exaggeration, like, "She does not properly dress the children." (Actually, they were well dressed, but she did let them run around barefoot in the hot summer.) Since love "does not take into account the wrong suffered" (1 Corinthians 13:5), Jack had violated his commitment to love Jane as Christ loved the church (Ephesians 5:25). In addition, he had disobeyed the injunction of 1 Corinthians 6 to not go before a pagan court to settle a dispute between believers.

Jane retaliated with accusations that were equally petty. The hatred generated in several hours of court testimony would rival anything that might be expected of pagans.

The court awarded the children to Jane, anyway. A short time later, Jane became severely aware of her deep sin and repented. She broke off her involvement with the other man, sought Christian counsel, and tried to repair the breach between herself and Jack. However, Jack, armed with the pontification of his pastor that he was "free," was already dating. Although he made an anemic attempt at reconciliation, he was never willing to admit he was wrong about anything he had said or done. He wanted Jane to bear the entire burden of the guilt. The bitterness left impassable barriers between them, and they went their separate ways.

Thinking back on this incident, I wonder what would have happened if Jack and his pastor had set out to heal rather than to wound, to restore rather than to retaliate, and to show the love of Christ rather than to demonstrate hostility.

People can say all they want about an "innocent party," but

who is really innocent? Both parties contribute, knowingly or unknowingly, to a marriage breakup. The major blame may be squarely on the shoulders of your mate, but you must confess to God your part in contributing, overtly or covertly, to the problem. If God points out sin in your life, your responsibility is to confess your sin. "If we confess [*homologeo* means "to say the same thing" or "agree"] our sins, He is faithful and righteous to forgive us our sins and to cleanse us from all unrighteousness" (1 John 1:9).

There is great stress in going through a divorce. According to the Stress Rating Chart, it is exceeded only by the death of a spouse, though more recently some social scientists are claiming that divorce is actually more stressful than losing a spouse through death. Since "divorce is one of the most devastating experiences undergone by human beings,"[1] it is not surprising that a lot of bitterness is found in its wake. In Hebrews 12:15 we read, "See to it that no one comes short of the grace of God; that no root of bitterness springing up causes trouble, and by it many be defiled." We cannot stress too strongly the importance of dealing with bitterness, anger, resentment, or vindictiveness as serious sin; if left unchecked, they will poison everything you do in future days. When we are out of fellowship with one another, it is often because we are out of fellowship with God.

Purpose to Present Yourself to God

Paul wrote: "I urge you therefore, brethren, by the mercies of God, to present your bodies a living and holy sacrifice, acceptable to God, which is your spiritual service of worship" (Romans 12:1).

Jesus Christ is Lord, and He desires that we commit ourselves to that lordship, submit our attitudes and actions to His control, and permit Him to have His way in our lives. The same word *present* is found twice in Romans 6:13.

And do not go on presenting the members of your body to sin as instruments of unrighteousness; but present yourselves to God as those alive from the dead, and your members as instruments of righteousness to God.

Our lips should be yielded to God so that the words we speak will build up rather than tear down (Ephesians 4:29). Our hands should be yielded to God so that the deeds we do will be good (Romans 12:20-21). Our feet should be yielded to God so that the paths we follow will be straight (Hebrews 12:13).

Each member of our bodies, from the top of our heads to the soles of our feet, should be committed to God to be used as an instrument of love and peace and hope to others, including our mates.

Fred was hurt by the legal action against him initiated by his ex-wife Katherine. She wanted more alimony and an improved settlement on their property. "She is trying to bleed me dry!" was his plaintive cry.

"Are you willing to be used of God as an instrument of love to her, Fred?"

"Yes, but what can I do?" It was a fresh spring day that Fred dropped to his knees in my office and said, "Lord, I yield my mouth, my hands, my life to you. Use me as an instrument of peace." Fred gave up his rights to any claim on the property. He promised to pay all Kathy asked, and he told her the reason was that God wanted His love to be expressed to her through him.

Before Christmas that same year, I had the joy of reuniting Fred and Kathy. She could resist Fred's animosity, but she could not escape Christ's love. Is your body available to Christ for anything He desires?

Purpose to Seek Reconciliation

High on God's list of priorities is the matter of reconciliation. Provision is not only made for reconciliation between a Holy

God and sinful man (2 Corinthians 5:18-21; Romans 5:10), but also between a husband and a wife (1Corinthians 7:11). The verb used in both cases means "to change" and implies a change from enmity to friendship. Another form of the same word is used in Ephesians 2:16 along with a second word that is virtually synonymous with the idea of reconciliation—peace. In the New Testament, the concept of peace is inseparably linked with its Hebrew counterpart *shalom,* which means "wholeness, oneness, and unity." Thus in Acts 7:26 the KJV translates peace, "to set at one again" and the NASB translates it "to reconcile them in peace."

When you insert that translation into 1 Corinthians 7:15 you have: "But God has called us to [reconcile them in] peace." This is in a context where the husband or wife who is a believer has been separated at the insistence of the unbelieving partner. The believer is told that he or she "is not under bondage in such cases." All that means is that "he or she need not feel so bound by Christ's prohibition of divorce as to be afraid to depart when the heathen partner insists on separation."[2] Following that statement is the contrast, "but God has called us to peace." This would seem to parallel the admonition to reconciliation in 1 Corinthians 7:11.

We say all of this to bring home an important point. If you want to please God, you must give high priority to full reconciliation. "If possible, so far as it depends upon you, be at peace with all men" (Romans 12:18). That means that you should exhaust all your options to find peace. It ultimately requires the cooperation of both partners to establish unity, but you should go the second mile and beyond to bring about the reconciliation. Just remember how far God went to reconcile you to Himself.

In Romans 14:18-19, in a context of Christian charity toward the weaker brother, Paul says, "For he who in this way serves Christ is acceptable [well pleasing] to God and approved by men. So then let us pursue the things which make for peace and the building up of one another." To build bridges of reconciliation rather than walls of retaliation is pleasing to God. In the Beatitudes Christ said, "Blessed are the peacemakers, for they shall be called sons of God" (Matthew 5:9). And Paul wrote to the Corinthian church, "Live in peace; and the God of love and peace shall be with you" (2 Corinthians 13:11). In the light of Christ's soon return, he wrote, "Live in peace with one another" (1 Thessalonians 5:13).

Although these admonitions are to all Christians, they have special application to those who are not only one in Christ as believers, but one flesh. And they also apply to the person with an unbelieving mate. For the sake of the testimony and for the sake of pleasing God, seek reconciliation. "For how do you know, O wife, whether you will save your husband? Or how do you know, O husband, whether you will save your wife?" (1 Corinthians 7:16)

Purpose to Please Your Mate
In the process of reconciliation, a Christian man or woman must seek to set the relationship on a new course. As long as you are not asked to do anything that displeases God, you should devote yourself to pleasing your marriage partner.

This should also hold true if there is separation involved. While you are not "enslaved" (1 Corinthians 7:15, KJV), you can choose to please that person to bring healing to the relationship. Keep in mind that before a divorce a couple is still married, even if they are not living together. Thus the same standard applies to a separated couple as to a married couple. "But one who is married is concerned about the things of the world, how he may please his wife. . . . But one who is married is concerned about the things of the world, how she may please her husband" (1 Corinthians 7:33-34).

God expects married people to give priority to pleasing their partners. This may prove difficult where there has been the breaking down of communication and building up of hostilities; yet, to please God you must make an effort. A practical suggestion might be to make a list of your mate's likes and dislikes and then systematically try to fulfill the desires and avoid the things that are not enjoyed.

Dr. Ed Wheat in his helpful chapter, "How to Save Your Marriage Alone,"[3] has twenty-two excellent suggestions. And Dr. Wayne Mack, In *A Homework Manual for Biblical Counseling,*[4] has a list of thirty-five things a husband can do to please his wife and that many that a wife can do to please her husband. These involve things such as showing leadership, buying flowers, fixing a nice meal, or cleaning the house.

Having determined what is pleasing to your partner, follow through. In order to do that, it is essential that there be self-denial. It is axiomatic that you cannot please both yourself and others at the same time. Christ declared that to follow Him one must "deny himself" (Matthew 16:24; Mark 8:34). "Now we who are strong ought to bear the weaknesses of those without strength and not just please ourselves. Let each of us please his neighbor for his good, to his edification. For even Christ did not please Himself" (Romans 15:1-3).

One of the biggest hindrances to restoring a marriage relationship is the unwillingness of a spouse to say no to his desires in order to reach out and care for his mate. If you want to please God, you will put your marriage partner ahead of yourself.

Purpose to Forgive and Seek Forgiveness

Forgiveness is a key word in reconciliation. You are to learn to "confess your sins to one another . . . so you may be healed" (James 5:16). Not only that, but when you come before God to worship and there remember that you have an unresolved conflict, you are to "first be reconciled to your brother" and then continue your worship (Matthew 5:23-24). True worship of God can be effective only if interpersonal conflicts are resolved. It is tragic but true that a very high percentage of marital conflicts are left unresolved. The people just walk away and steel their conscience against any response. They say, "I don't care anymore." But God does, and He demands that we have " a blameless conscience both before God and before men" (Acts 24:16).

Even if your situation seems hopeless,

• Forgive your partner of any wrong done to you (Ephesians 4:32).

• Realize how you contributed to the failure of the marriage, even if it was a very small thing (Psalm 139:23-24).

• Confess the sin to God (1 John 1:9).

• If at all possible, communicate your fault to your partner, asking his or her forgiveness. Be specific (James 5:16).

• Be prepared for further rejection. The mate may say, "I'll never forgive you," but you can rest on the fact that you did what was pleasing to God.

In dealing with hundreds of couples over the years, I have repeatedly heard the words, "I could never forgive her," or, "I could never forgive him." The passage of Scripture that I refer them to most often is Matthew 18:21-35. It is significant that this admonition comes between Christ's teaching on the proper procedure of seeking reconciliation by church discipline (Matthew 18:15-20) and the well-known divorce passage (Matthew 19:1-12). Peter posed a question, "Lord, how often shall my brother sin against me and I forgive him?" He then offered to be gracious by suggesting "up to seven times." Christ shocked him by increasing that amount seventy-fold to 490 times. This means there is no limit to what we should forgive.

To reinforce His point, Jesus told a parable. A king forgave his servant an enormous sum—a debt he could never pay. That same servant encountered a fellow-servant who owed him a petty amount and demanded instant payment.

The application is clear: We accumulated a debt of sin we could never pay. Our guilt before God was enormous. God provided His Son, Jesus Christ, and paid the debt for us, forgiving the tresspasses that were against us (Colossians 2:13). Yet so often, when another person incurs a debt by committing a sin against us, we are unwilling to forgive. Paul instructed the Ephesian Christians: "And be kind to one another, tender-hearted, forgiving each other, just as God in Christ also has forgiven you" (Ephesians 4:32). This is pleasing to God.

Purpose to Pray for Your Partner

"Pray for one another, so that you may be healed. The effective prayer of a righteous man can accomplish much" (James 5:16). When a person prays in the will of God, guided by the Word of God, and empowered by the Spirit of God, things begin to happen. We all claim to believe in prayer, but we show little of the persistence in prayer taught in the New Testament. There are times we are hesitant to pray dogmatically about a matter because we cannot be sure what is God's best; but in this matter of the restoration of a broken home, there can be no doubt as to what He desires. We should pray with an earnest, beseeching heart that God will do a miracle in the family. He can, you know! "You do not have because you do not ask" (James 4:2). We must learn to keep on asking, keep on seeking, keep on knocking. The result will be receiving, finding, and the opening of doors (Matthew 7:7-8).

When Reconciliation Is Impossible

The discussion in this chapter so far has assumed that reconciliation may be possible. But what if one or both partners have remarried? Even though we are convinced that remarriage after a divorce is always wrong as long as the former partner is alive, we are equally convinced that when remarriage has taken place, God expects that relationship to continue. There is no point in breaking up one's present family in order to try to undo the past. If it is best to remain in the present relationship, then obviously full reconciliation with one's former mate is impossible. This situation would then require some different priorities.

A person should still:

• Purpose to get right with God. If you have remarried, this would include the acknowledgment of the remarriage as sin. There is no sense in justifying it. God calls it sin; so must we.

• Purpose to present yourself to God. God is in the business of taking broken lives and making them useful. Be available to Him as an instrument to His glory.

• Purpose to forgive completely the hurt of your former marriage and seek forgiveness from your former partner, just as in the case where reconciliation is possible.

• Purpose to ask forgiveness of your present mate (if remarried) for causing him or her to sin by marrying you.

Homer, a Christian businessman, came for counseling. There was a sense of strain between him and Mary, his wife of five years, and he feared that their relationship was headed the same way as his first marriage. After listening to his rather lengthy story and sharing with him what Scripture says about divorce and remarriage, I suggested three steps.

First, confess to God your sin of contributing to the divorce and the sin of remarriage. Second, communicate to your ex-wife your fault in the marriage breakup and seek her forgiveness. Third, ask Mary to forgive you for your sin in persuading her to marry you, a divorced man.

Two weeks later Homer returned to say there was no improvement. When asked if he had taken the suggested steps, he replied, "I did the first two, but I cannot do the third because it would just hurt Mary and make matters worse." I pointed out, "He who conceals his transgressions will not prosper" (Proverbs 28:13), and insisted that his admission of guilt could remove barriers and open channels of communications between him and Mary.

A few days later Homer called. "Pastor," he said, "you will never believe what happened." His story tumbled out.

I finally got up enough courage to talk to Mary last night. I told her I had come to you for counsel. I wanted her to know that I loved her, that I would be her husband forever, but that I had learned that it is wrong to divorce and wrong to remarry. I told her that I had confessed this sin to God, to my ex-wife, and now I was asking for her forgiveness for leading her into sin.

Mary jumped to her feet, ran into the bedroom, threw herself across the bed, and began weeping convulsively. I thought, "What have I done now? I never should have listened to that fool preacher." I entered the bedroom and tried to comfort her, assuring her of my love.

When she calmed down, she startled me with these words: "Homer, I want to thank you. You will never know what a relief this is." Then she shared with me the fact that her pastor had counseled her against marrying a divorced man. Insistent on having her own way, she found another pastor who would perform the simple ceremony. She admitted that for five years she had been tortured with guilt for her sin, but was afraid to admit it was sin to either God or me, because she did not want to hurt me. Now she was free to confess her willful sin and get right with God.

Homer and Mary are happily married now, with all barriers gone, and are living productive Christian lives.

If you are divorced and have not remarried, but your partner has, the door is closed for reconciliation; but God still has a plan for your life. When you have confessed your sin and cleared your conscience, you must purpose not to remarry but to make yourself available to help others to learn the lessons you have learned through harsh experience. Like the single person of 1 Corinthians 7:32, you can be concerned about the things of the Lord. You can be available to God as an instrument of healing in the broken homes around you. You can be used of God to give a word of caution to young people who are rushing into marriage. You can be displayed as a trophy of God's grace— still suffering for sin, but now suffering according to God's will (1 Peter 4:19). Life does not end with the misfortune of divorce. For the person who is willing to please God there are always new heights, new horizons, and new hope. May it be said of you as it was of Enoch, "He obtained the witness . . . he was pleasing to God" (Hebrews 11:5).

FOOTNOTES

1. Raymond E. Vath and Daniel W. O'Neill, *Marrying for Life,* (Bothell, Washington: Messenger Communications, 1981), p. 21.
2. Archibald Robertson and Alfred Plummer, *A Critical and Exegetical Commentary on the First Epistle of Paul to the Corinthians,* 2nd ed., The International Critical Commentary, (Edinburgh: T. & T. Clark, 1911), p. 145.
3. Ed Wheat, *Love Life for Every Married Couple,* (Grand Rapids: Zondervan Publishing House, 1980), pp. 203-228.
4. Wayne Mack, *A Homework Manual for Biblical Counseling,* Vol. 2, (Phillipsburg, N.J.: Presbyterian & Reformed Publishing Co., 1980), pp. 21-25.

12

The Divorced
Person in the Church

Despite the rampant divorce rate, there is an encouraging trend. Strong voices proclaiming God's standard of righteousness are being heard in the land. Increasing numbers of books and articles are upholding God's idea of permanence in marriage. Men of the caliber of F.F. Bruce and Gordon Wenham, and young scholars such as Carl Laney and Bill Heth, are urging evangelicals to take a new look at this issue. Across our nation courageous pastors are admitting that they have been wrong and are refusing to encourage divorce or to marry previously divorced persons.

A recent Gallup poll for *Christianity Today* revealed that a surprising percentage of Americans still believe divorce should be avoided under all circumstances and that remarriage after divorce is acceptable only in cases where the former mate is dead. The survey covered the full spectrum of denominations, both liberal and conservative theological persuasions. It showed that evangelical clergy, persons who have had a conversion experience, those who are frequent Bible readers and frequent churchgoers take a more conservative view than others. For example: twenty-seven percent of frequent Bible readers believe that remarriage following divorce is never permitted and twenty-five percent of Baptists (other than Southern Baptists) do not believe divorce is ever justified.[1]

The poll is discussed by William M. Kinnaird, who warns against pastors picking and choosing which of God's laws they will honor. He quotes Pastor Steve Brown of Key Biscayne Presbyterian Church as saying,

> I believe that God has never affirmed divorce. This includes Christians and non-Christians. Marriage is a part of the Adamic covenant and is therefore binding on everyone. . . . I never even suggest divorce as an alternative because it isn't one. I show couples what the Bible says (Malachi 2:16; Matthew 19) and let them know that no matter how bad their situation, God is perfectly capable of restoring their marriage. Divorce is sin.[2]

Theologian R. C. Sproul says,

> Civil courts are disrupting the commandments of God in granting illicit divorces. In many cases the institutional church has sanctioned divorce (and remarriage) on the grounds that are in clear opposition to the teachings of Christ. Clergymen and counselors through the land are recommending divorce (and permitting remarriage) where Christ had prohibited it. It means that not only is the sanctity of marriage corrupted by both the state and the church, but that the authority of Christ is flagrantly disobeyed in both spheres over which He is King. The word for such disobedience is treason.[3]

While both Sproul and Brown apparently hold to the Erasmian view of remarriage, they are to be commended for their strong antidivorce stance. Perhaps a new day has dawned and the tide of divorce can be stemmed, offering hope for the generation of tomorrow.

Divorced Persons in the Church

Meanwhile, we face another question that must be answered today. What is the place of the divorced person in the church?

In years past when divorce was rare among believers, the church took an extremely negative, even sometimes noncompassionate, view of the divorcee. They seemed to join secular society in stigmatizing such a person. While this was not in keeping with the restoring, reconciling, and forgiving mission of God's people, it did not pose too great a problem numerically, since so few were involved.

Today, however, a large percentage of those involved in our churches have experienced the misfortune of divorce and many of these are already remarried. In California where the divorce rate is well ahead of the national average, it is not unusual to find fifty percent to seventy-five percent of the adults in a church having had a divorce in their past. Exactly where do these folks fit in the ministry of their local church? Can they serve at all? Are there limits? What is their place?

We state unequivocally that God forgives all sin, and that includes the sins of divorce and remarriage. A person who persists in upholding his right to violate scriptural principles may be subject to both God's chastening hand (Hebrews 12:6; Proverbs 29:1) and the discipline of the local church (Matthew 18:15-17). But when a person acknowledges his sin and comes to God in repentence, God fully restores that one to Himself, and he should be restored to the local church as well. Sin, however, does leave scars, and the consequences of sin do not automatically disappear even when the sin itself has been forgiven.

David repented of his sin in deep contrition (Psalm 51), but his child still died (2 Samuel 12:16-20). He reaped grim consequences both in his family (2 Samuel 13—15) and in his kingdom. David was called a man after God's own heart (Acts 13:22), but his past sin left him with limitations on his life.

Moses is another example (Numbers 20:1-13). He led the people to the edge of the Promised Land; but because of one rash act he was not allowed to lead them in. It may seem grossly unfair to keep a man from his ultimate goal because of one moment of sin, but in the economy of God the most important thing is the exhibition of God's glory, not the fulfilling of man's desires. Moses pled with God to change His mind and allow him to enter, but God said no (Deuteronomy 3:24-26). Moses' sin was a failure to act in accordance with the specific word of God. God said, "Speak to the rock"; Moses took matters into his own hands and broke faith with God.

Not only that, but Moses failed to demonstrate the uniquely holy nature of God. "But the Lord said to Moses and Aaron, 'Because you have not believed Me, to treat Me as holy in the sight of the sons of Israel, therefore you shall not bring this assembly into the land which I have given them'" (Numbers 20:12). Note the words, "treat Me as Holy." God's servant was expected to respond in keeping with the character of God. When he did not, God demonstrated His holiness by divine discipline on Moses. "And He proved Himself holy among them" (Numbers 20:13). Implicit in this story is another reason for the strict judgment of Moses. It was God's intention to use the striking of the rock at Rephidim (Exodus 17:1-7) as an illustration of Christ's death and apparently to use the speaking to the rock at Kadesh (Numbers 20:1-13) as an illustration of His intercessory ministry (see 1 Corinthians 10:4). There was far more involved here than a momentary rise of temper. Moses by one act did damage to God's purpose.

This can be applied to the problem of divorce. Remember that marriage is an illustration of the relationship between Christ and the church (Ephesians 5:22-33). Divorce spoils the illustration and defaces the picture. Once a divorce has taken place, perhaps followed by remarriage to another partner, the typology is marred. It is not surprising then that limitations are placed on the divorced person when it comes to service in the local church. To ignore the fact of divorce would be to ignore the priority God has placed on the permanence of marriage and the high qualifications the Bible sets for church leadership.

The 1982 General Conference of the Evangelical Free Church

adopted a policy forbidding the licensing or ordination of those who are divorced or married to one who has been divorced.[4]

We contacted ninety mission boards serving the foreign field. Over one-half would not consider divorced people for career missionaries; over one-third would not accept divorced candidates for short-term service; and nearly twenty percent would not even consider divorced people for home staff (secretaries, accountants, etc.). Most of the missions responding indicated that under ordinary circumstances, divorce is a serious disqualifying factor to a missionary candidate.

While expressing genuine concern for divorced persons and their place of future service, these missions believe that career missionaries must have a standard that is equivalent to the qualifications of pastor or elder (Titus 1:5-9; 1 Timothy 3:1-7). Many stated that the standard about divorce is much stricter in the mission churches than in the churches of the United States. A number stressed the value of the missionary's marriage as a role model.

Dr. Earl Radmacher recently pointed out that even handicapped people were restricted in the Levitical system, not because God didn't like the handicapped, but because of the special nature of the priesthood which:

> ... not only served to illustrate Yahweh's transcendence, but served on the level of redemptive analogy as well. Yahweh desired to portray that his ultimate mediator, Jesus Christ, must be perfect in all respects. In this symbolization it was necessary to have these acts done by physically perfect priests.[5]

He points out that a priest could not marry a divorced woman or a widow, and then applies this to the standard of blamelessness required of leaders in the church. He concludes,

> If divorced and remarried men were permitted to serve in the highest office of the church, their marriages would inaccurately represent the indissoluble relationship between Christ and the church.[6]

On the biblical basis of qualification for leadership, those who have had marriage failure and those who further have complicated the issue by remarriage may be considered disqualified for certain ministries. These passages spell out that the leader must be above reproach, meeting specific family requirements. No one should be able to bring an accusation about anything in the life of a leader that might compromise the testimony of the body.

The attitude a divorced person should display should be like Moses when he realized he could not enter the Promised Land. He served God the rest of his days and left behind a heritage and legacy for the next generation. It is exciting to hear of a divorced person, who has learned that he cannot serve as a pastor or a missionary or elder because of his past marriage failure, saying, "If I cannot go, I'll pray and give so others can."

Just a few weeks ago a teenager in our church told me he had a new appreciation for marriage. He had asked his father why he was not an elder and his father explained that because of the past sin of divorce and remarriage, he was restricted. The wise father then told his son that he must treat marriage with the sacredness which God gives it. The young man said, "I am going to be very careful whom I date and eventually marry because I can't afford to mess up. There is too much at stake."

All of us must accept our limitations. One person may have a physical disability; another may have something in his background, like a police record, that would limit him in some way. Your disability may be your fault, or you may be the innocent victim of circumstances beyond your control.

Stan had committed himself to becoming a missionary, but at the end of his senior year of high school he got in with the wrong crowd. One night he was arrested with his friends in a stolen car. Stan did not know the car was stolen nor that in the trunk were stolen goods which were linked to the death of a night watchman.

Though innocent himself, Stan could not prove it; he was

tried as an adult and convicted of felony manslaughter. After five years in prison, he went to Bible school and continued to pursue his goal of becoming a missionary. But to his dismay he learned that it is virtually impossible for a convicted felon to get a resident visa in a foreign country. His hopes were shattered and he became very despondent until he faced and accepted his limitation and determined to serve God in any way He might lead. He was never able to go to the mission field, but he has done his part for missions here at home.

We share Stan's story because we want to encourage divorced people to realize that they are not the only ones who experience limitations on their service. Being disqualified for one kind of service can open a door to serving God in some other way. God loves you and will forgive you. He has not given up on you and will still use you. Even your limitations will serve to prove the Lord "holy among them" (Numbers 20:13). His grace is sufficient for you (2 Corinthians 12:9).

How Can the Divorced Serve?

What then can a divorced person do? First, the church should not stigmatize the divorced person by making him a second-class Christian. Where it has done this, it has been wrong. When a person has shown true repentence over past sin and a firm resolve to agree with God's Word on the subject of divorce, many ministries should be available to him.

It is the responsibility of all Christians to witness, give, pray, and encourage others. You may have opportunities to counsel and visit the sick, serve widows, help the handicapped, write letters to missionaries, or work in telephone-contact ministries and tape ministries. There are volunteer opportunities in the local rescue mission or convalescent hospital. You can be involved in a home Bible study under the leadership of your church. Ushering and singing in the choir provide opportunities, as do typing and clerical work. You may even have the opportunity of going to the mission field on a short-term service assignment.

I suggest you go to your pastor and be open and honest with him. Tell him you have been divorced. Assure him that you do not approve of divorce and that you have confessed it as sin. Inform him that you know there are limits as to your service, but that you have accepted your limitations and want to serve God in any way you can. Ask him what ministries are open to you in that church. While the opportunities will vary from church to church, you will be surprised at the open doors you will find when your heart is willing to serve God.

Don't overlook the ministry you can have to those contemplating divorce or remarriage. Your testimony and experience may be just what is needed to head off someone who is about to make a serious mistake. When a divorced person sees marriage failure as sin and remarriage as further sin, he wields a powerful influence over those who are about to give up. Let God use you as an instrument of warning and reconciliation.

Finally, one of your greatest ministries is that of being an example to the next generation. Your heartache and even your limitations will send a message to them that the cost of sin is high; and that even though it is forgiven, there are continuing consequences. If God has blessed you with children, you will teach them volumes as you deny yourself and your desires and concentrate on serving God within your limitations. You will be used of God to sound a warning to today's young people. The message will come as a certain sound.

> What God has called sacred, don't call profane. What God has set apart, don't make common. What God has joined together, let no man separate.
> Satan's way of disharmony, disunity, and divorce leads only to heartache. Keep a high view of marriage, build your life around the purposes of God, and don't allow compromise of His principles. Let Christ be Lord of your life, Lord of your future, Lord of your marriage.

This message is much needed today, and who is better able

to declare it than you who have learned through bitter experiences the tragedy of divorce? There is hope for the divorce generation.

FOOTNOTES

1. William M. Kinnaird, "Divorce and Remarriage: Ministers in the Middle," *Christianity Today,* June 6, 1980, pp. 24-27.
2. Ibid.
3. Ibid.
4. "Conference Approves Policy on Ministerial Divorce," *The Evangelical Beacon,* July 1982, pp. 10-11.
5. Earl Radmacher, "President's Corner," *Western Communicator,* Summer 1982, p. 2.
6. Ibid.

A Concluding Word

There is hardly a person in our country today who has not been touched in one way or another by the tragedy of divorce. Some have gone through the experience of a parent or child being divorced; for others it has been another relative or a close friend. Divorce has become so common that it is accepted as inevitable by much of the evangelical community.

In his *Essay on Man,* Alexander Pope wrote:

Vice is a monster of so frightful mien
As to be hated needs but to be seen;
Yet seen too oft, familiar with her face,
We first endure, then pity, then embrace.

There is the everpresent danger that when sin becomes commonplace it will soon be accepted as normal. Satan has so successfully duped people into compromise that what was disdained in a previous generation is accepted as legitimate by this generation. Because of the strategic nature of the home and family, and because of its inseparable link to the life and ministry of the church, we must not tolerate this acceptance with regard to divorce and remarriage.

If the deterioration is allowed to continue, Satan may soon

be successful in eliminating qualified leadership in our churches. If that happens, then the church will lose its impact in the world.

Perhaps you are asking, "How can I help?" Let us offer a few practical suggestions.

1. Commit yourself to the standards of Scripture. Then live them without compromise.

2. Make known those standards in a spirit of Christian love and concern. Many people do not really know what the Bible teaches on these subjects.

3. Give some of your time to help save marriages. Regretably, some attorneys, psychologists, and Christian counselors offer advice that tends to break up Christian homes. We need Christians who will help reconcile and restore.

4. Use your influence to encourage biblical standards for leadership in the church. Help present leaders to evaluate themselves and potential leaders by the standards of 1 Timothy 3 and Titus 1.

5. Encourage a ministry to divorced people in your church which will help them focus on spiritual growth and productivity rather than on remarriage. Give them hope and direction.

6. Never allow yourself to become complacent about this problem which is worsening every year.

7. Talk to your pastor about your concern. Even those of the Erasmian persuasion are deeply troubled about the condition of things today, because they are constantly confronted with the heartbreak of divorce. Perhaps you can encourage your pastor to reexamine the biblical teaching and take a firm stand against divorce and remarriage.

8. Pray that the Lord who instituted marriage will bring healing and reconciliation to the troubled homes you know about.

It has been our desire in this book to try to thwart Satan's attacks against the Christian home. We have written with burdened hearts that are jealous to maintain the standards of the Word of God and yet sensitive and tender toward the needs of

God's people. We hope we have ploughed some fresh soil and have planted seeds which will bring forth fruit to His glory.